Making
work work

by Marcus Nodder

Making work work
The good book guide to work
© Marcus Nodder/The Good Book Company, 2013.
Series Consultants: Tim Chester, Tim Thornborough,
                    Anne Woodcock, Carl Laferton

The Good Book Company
Tel (UK): 0333 123 0880
Tel: (US): 866 244 2165
Tel (int): + (44) 208 942 0880
Email: info@thegoodbook.co.uk / sales@thegoodbook.com

Websites
UK: www.thegoodbook.co.uk
North America: www.thegoodbook.com
Australia: www.thegoodbook.com.au
New Zealand: www.thegoodbook.co.nz

ISBN: 9781908762894

Printed in China

CONTENTS

introduction: good book guides

Every Bible-study group is different—yours may take place in a church building, in a home or in a cafe, on a train, over a leisurely mid-morning coffee or squashed into a 30-minute lunch break. Your group may include new Christians, mature Christians, non-Christians, mums and tots, students, businessmen or teens. That's why we've designed these *Good Book Guides* to be flexible for use in many different situations.

Our aim in each session is to uncover the meaning of a passage, and see how it fits into the "big picture" of the Bible. But that can never be the end. We also need to appropriately apply what we have discovered to our lives. Let's take a look at what is included:

Talkabout: Most groups need to "break the ice" at the beginning of a session, and here's the question that will do that. It's designed to get people talking around a subject that will be covered in the course of the Bible study.

Investigate: The Bible text for each session is broken up into manageable chunks, with questions that aim to help you understand what the passage is about. **The Leader's Guide** contains **guidance on questions**, and sometimes ⊻ additional "follow-up" questions.

Explore more (optional): These questions will help you connect what you have learned to other parts of the Bible, so you can begin to fit it all together like a jig-saw; or occasionally look at a part of the passage that's not dealt with in detail in the main study.

Apply: As you go through a Bible study, you'll keep coming across **apply** sections. These are questions to get the group discussing what the Bible teaching means in practice for you and your church. **Getting personal** is an opportunity for you to think, plan and pray about the changes that you personally may need to make as a result of what you have learned.

Pray: We want to encourage prayer that is rooted in God's word—in line with His concerns, purposes and promises. So each session ends with an opportunity to review the truths and challenges highlighted by the Bible study, and turn them into prayers of request and thanksgiving.

The **Leader's Guide** and introduction provide historical background information, explanations of the Bible texts for each session, ideas for **optional extra** activities, and guidance on how best to help people uncover the truths of God's word.

why study *Making work work*?

Most of us spend most of our waking hours at work. It takes up most of our energy and often most of our emotions. It is at times really fulfilling, and at other times utterly frustrating. It keeps a roof over our heads and food on our tables... but is there any more to work than that?

In *Snow White*, the seven dwarves sing: "We dig up diamonds by the score, a thousand rubies, sometimes more; we don't know what we dig them for... Hi ho, hi ho, it's home from work we go." Like them, we are often a little confused about why we go to work, apart from to earn money. Christians can feel that what they do Monday to Friday is irrelevant to their faith; or, worse, gets in the way of them living out their faith. Others who don't go to work in an office or factory can feel that they are of little worth.

Could work—should work—be anything more than something to go to, make money at, and return home from?

The Bible's answer is: *Yes!* In these eight studies, we'll see what work is, and why we find work in this world alternately fulfilling and frustrating. We'll see how to approach the money we make, the people we work with, and the worries we have in a godly way.

And we'll see that the ultimate worker is not you, or me, but Jesus Christ; that the Christian life is not so much a life of work, but a life of enjoying Christ's work for us.

Whether you go out to work, or are a parent whose work is at home... whether you're out of work, starting your first job, running a company, or retired... these studies will show you, excite you and challenge you with God's perspective on working in His world.

1

Genesis 1 v 26 – 2 v 25

PURPOSE AT WORK

⊕ talkabout

1. How would you define work?

A job you do. Paid & unpaid. FT or PT. Not location bound.

• What is the point of work?

Do you think?

⊥ investigate

> **Read Genesis 1 v 26-28**

2. What task does God give mankind to do? What do you think that means?

Rule by lovingly care for the world just as God does.

DICTIONARY

Image (v 26, 27): reflection, character.
Rule over (v 26): be in charge of and care for something lovingly.
Be fruitful (v 27): have children.

> **Read Genesis 2 v 4-15**

3. What particular job does God give Adam to do? How is this part of his God-given task?

Gardening! – work was 1 way to rule.

Also includes dominion.

4. How do God's work and man's work go together (v 5, 8, 15)?

God began the work for Adam to take on.
We work under Gods ultimate rule

→ **apply**

5. Jesus told us to pray: "Give us each day our daily bread" (Luke 11 v 3). But how do God's work and human work need to come together before we find a loaf of bread in our kitchen?

Even the food God provides is a collaborative effort.

6. Work is part of God's flawless, original creation. How should this shape our attitude to our work?

work in itself is not a curse.
Humans work, Its in our DNA
work = obeying/serving God.

• How does it help us understand why being unemployed can be so hard?

7. Put the following jobs in order of importance: car mechanic, missionary, refuse collector, doctor, shop assistant, banker, teacher, church leader, brain surgeon.

- As Christians, does it matter what job we do?

No. How we do it is far more important.

☺ getting personal

Where does the work you do fit into the bigger picture of enabling the world to function as God intended? Is this how you view it from day to day?

How often do you pray about your work? What does this say about your view of it, and of yourself?

☺ explore more

optional

▶ **Read Luke 3 v 12-14**

"Christians working in banking or the Armed Forces should do something more worthwhile instead, such as becoming doctors or teachers." *What do these verses say to this idea?*

▶ **Read Mark 6 v 3**

Some people look down on those who do manual work (eg: builders or mechanics). Why, do you think? What does this verse say to that? Imagine a Christian teenager asks you how they should decide what job to do. What advice would you give them?

⊥ investigate

▶ **Read Genesis 2 v 18-25**

8. What does God say is not good? How does He solve the problem?

Loneliness & solo work.

Creates companion & helper.

9. What does 1 v 28 suggest is one purpose of marriage? How does this help humanity "rule over" the earth?!

Need more goodness! ∴ Raising family is key in Gods work

→ apply

10. What do people in our society think of the work of bearing children, raising a family and running a home compared to "pursuing a career"? How similar or different is this to God's view?

world says "only a mother"

11. How might we use our work as an excuse for neglecting our marriage (or vice versa)?

12. Sum up what we've learned about the ultimate point of work. What is the key truth you will take away from this study?

Cutty Stone.
Earing e living
Build a Cathedral

⊡ getting personal

If someone asked you: "How are you serving God at the moment?", what would you say? Do you see your daily work as one way in which you serve Him? What difference would it make if you did?

No one job is more valuable to God than another. How does this encourage you, and challenge you, in your current job?

Are you in more danger of ignoring your family to focus on your job, or using family as an excuse to neglect your job? How will you make sure you do neither?

⊕ pray

Thank God:

• for the gift of work and the wonderful variety of jobs there is.

• for the privilege of ruling the world under Him and the part work plays in this.

• for the "work of the home" and the "work of the garden" and your work in one, or the other, or both.

Ask God:

• for help to see your work as part of how you serve Him.

• for help to have a biblical view of the "work of the home".

• for a thankful spirit at work, even on Monday morning!

2 Genesis 3; 4; 11; 31
TROUBLE AT WORK

The story so far

Our daily work, inside or outside the home, is part of God's good design for us, ruling the world under Him. So it is all valuable and worthwhile. ✳

⊕ talkabout

1. Share any holiday experiences you have had (or heard about) when the reality didn't live up to what you'd expected from the brochure.

    Holidays from Hell. My brother turned up to the 'beach view' hotel & the beach had been painted on a huge wall!

    • In the very good world of Genesis 1 – 2, Adam would have leaped out of bed on Monday morning, excited by the prospect of another week serving God as he worked in the garden. In what ways does your experience of work not always (or ever!) match that glossy brochure?!

    Why does 'good work' sometimes feel hard or bad of a punishment?

⊕ investigate

In Genesis 3, Adam and Eve rebelled against God, disobeying Him. As a result, God's judgment fell on them, and on the whole world. Everything was affected, including work. In this session, we'll see five ways that God's good design for work has been distorted because of human sin and God's judgment of it.

⌄ Trouble one

❯ Read Genesis 3 v 16-19a

2. In what ways did the "work of the home" become painful for the woman?

[handwritten] Being fruitful & multiplying will now hurt!

DICTIONARY

Desire (v 16): a drive to dominate and control someone (see 4 v 7).

- In what ways did the "work of the garden" become painful for the man?

[handwritten] The gift of work now cursed. Producing bad fruit & requiring more effort than before

⌄ Trouble two

❯ Read Genesis 3 v 19b and Ecclesiastes 1 v 2-4

3. Part of God's judgment on mankind was death. What impact does knowing we will die one day have on how we see our work day by day?

[handwritten] Seems meaningless when death is on horizon

⌄ Trouble three

❯ Read Genesis 4 v 3-8; 6 v 5

4. Why did Cain kill his brother?

[handwritten] angry jealous. Sin spoilt relationships!

⊕ apply

The site of the first murder was Cain and Abel's "workplace"—the field.

5. How do things like anger, envy, and hatred reveal themselves in your workplaces?

is the workplace harder than the work?

⊡ getting personal

Does the way you are treating others at work need to change in any way? Are there sins in your heart which are being expressed at work in how you relate to others?

Read through Jesus' list of heart sins in Mark 7 v 21-23 to help you see how this might be happening.

⊕ investigate

☑ Trouble four

▶ Read Genesis 11 v 1-9

6. What was these people's ambition in building this tower (v 4)?

Fruitfulness & submission was 'unto god'
this is above god or instead of him!?

• What was wrong about this (look back at 1 v 26-28)?

→ apply

7. How do people try to make themselves a reputation through work today?

we looked at our part in bigger picture but we aren't satisfied being a part.

- What adverse effects of this "tower-building" have you seen?

for tim it pushes god out completly

⊡ getting personal

Is there any aspect of your work where you're driven by making a name for yourself, rather than serving your Lord?

How is work (or could work be) in danger of taking God's place in your life?

What difference would it make to pray as you go to work:

"My Father in heaven, hallowed be your name—not mine.

Your kingdom come—not mine.

Your will be done—not mine. Amen."

↓ investigate

◗ Trouble five

▶ Read Genesis 31 v 38-42

Jacob, the grandson of Abraham, whose family God has promised to bless, is working for Laban, his uncle. Here, he is speaking to Laban.

8. In what ways was Jacob's working life unfair? What kept him going?

Cheated by employer

→ apply

9. Can you relate at all to his experience? How did you (or were you tempted to) react?

⊡ explore more

optional

> **Read Genesis 39 v 6b-20**

Jacob's son, Joseph, is a slave in Egypt.

How was Joseph unfairly treated at work because he obeyed God?

> **Read 1 Peter 2 v 18-23**

How does the example of Christ encourage us when we are unfairly treated at work?

10. Look back over this whole study. Why do you think it is important to be realistic about the difficulties of working life in a fallen world?

So we can face the problems clearly they inevitbly come

- Which of the five aspects of work in a fallen world can you relate to most? Have you learned anything from these passages that will help you deal with them next time?

⬆ pray

Thank God:

- that the Bible is so realistic about working life in a fallen world.
- that the Lord is with you in these difficulties.
- that work will be perfect again in the age to come, when God promises that: "my chosen ones will long enjoy the work of their hands. They will not labour in vain" (Isaiah 65 v 22-23).

Ask God:

- to strengthen people you know who are finding work especially difficult at the moment.
- to help you to keep serving Him in your work when it is hard.
- to help you be godly when you are under pressure at work (you might like to mention specific situations and challenges you are facing).

3 Ephesians 2; 4
SAVIOUR AT WORK

Saved by Jesus work.
Saved for work for Him

The story so far

Our daily work, inside or outside the home, is part of God's good design for us, ruling the world under Him. So it is all valuable and worthwhile.

This world is sinful, and under God's judgment. So work has been spoiled by pain, futility, broken relationships, godless ambition, and unfair treatment.

⊕ talkabout

1. If you did a street survey, what sort of answers would you get to the questions:

   • What is wrong with the world?

   • What is the solution?

⊕ investigate

   ▶ **Read Ephesians 2 v 1-10**

2. What is the spiritual condition of humanity (v 1-3)?

   Not enjoy like with God. DEAD!
   Not ruling ruled over! — world, sinful AA
   Devil.

   is this how we tnd to view ourselves?

DICTIONARY

Ruler of the kingdom of the air (v 2): the devil.
Wrath (v 3): God's right anger against sin.
Grace (v 5): undeserved love.

3. What has God done for Christians (v 4-7)? Why has He done this?

Saved us   made alive

united to the resurrected
Christ

By love

4. What do verses 8-10 emphasise about how we are saved; and about how we are *not* saved?

by Grace through faith.
Not by self works

5. What place do good works have in the Christian life (v 10)?

Able to do the work 1st intended.

➔ apply

6. How does this passage show us the limits of our own work (in the home, the office, the factory, our church, or anywhere else)?

Dead things can't rule.
Can't do what we were made to do
Can't save ourselves

⋯ getting personal

It's easy for Christians to drift back into feeling that their acceptance by God is based on their performance.

Do you feel that God is kinder to you when you have a "quiet time", but won't help you if you don't?

Do you ever feel guilty even when you've confessed your sins to God and turned from them?

You are saved by grace through faith alone, not through works. You cannot be any more loved by God than you already are. When do you most need to remember this?

⬇ investigate

God doesn't just save *individuals*. He joins us together as a *people*; He builds us up as His church. The church is a structure, built by God (2 v 18-22). And it is a body, grown by Him…

> **❯ Read Ephesians 4 v 4-16**

7. What is God's goal for the body?

Ligament (v 16): a body part which holds bones together.

> Growth.
> & maturity

8. What do God's people have (v 7-8)?

> All have grace, Gifts

- What do verses 11-12 tell us about what these are?

> to serve one another & to build up
> the whole

- How does the passage emphasise the importance of *every* Christian playing their part in their church?

> The body needs all its systems

9. The Bible calls this work of building up the church the "work of the Lord". **Read 1 Corinthians 15 v 58.** What should be our attitude to this work?

> Eternal sign ⟹ Not in vain.

⊡ explore more

> ▶ **Read Matthew 9 v 38**

What does Jesus say His "building project" (or harvest field) needs? What do we need to do?

> ▶ **Read 1 Corinthians 9 v 14**

What is one thing we should do for people who do this work as their paid job?

⊡ apply

The two main ways the body of Christ is built up is through edification (strengthening Christians) and evangelism (reaching out to non-Christians).

10. Why are both important?

- What happens in our local church if we neglect one in favour of the other?

- Which do you think your church could be (or is) more in danger of not pursuing? What can you do about this?

11. Why does the "work of the Lord" mean the Christian is never out of work?

12. How should this affect our view of:
   • unemployment?

   • retirement?

   • weekends?

⊼ pray

Thank God:

- for how He has worked through Christ to give us a place in His kingdom.
- for the good works He has prepared for us to do as His people.
- for the different gifts He has now given each member of your group to serve and build up the body of Christ, and for the opportunities He has given you to use them.

Ask God:

- to keep reminding you that you are saved by His grace, and not by any of your works.
- to show you how He wants you to be fully devoted to the "work of the Lord".
- to help your church leaders to be faithful in preparing you for service—and challenging you to get on with it!

4 Hebrews 3 v 7 – 4 v 11
REST FROM WORK

our rest now points to eternal rest

The story so far

Our daily work, inside or outside the home, is part of God's good design for us, ruling the world under Him. So it is all valuable and worthwhile.

This world is sinful, and under God's judgment. So work has been spoiled by pain, futility, broken relationships, godless ambition, and unfair treatment.

We are saved *by* Christ's work in His death and resurrection, not our own work. We are saved *for* working for God, doing good and building His church.

⊕ talkabout *Who's the most important?*

1. Find out what your own pace of life is by answering a few simple questions:

   (1) When someone takes too long to get to the point, do you hurry them along?

   (2) Are you the first person to finish at mealtimes?

   (3) When walking along a street, do you feel frustrated because you are stuck behind others?

   (4) Would you become irritable if you sat for an hour without doing anything?

   (5) Do you walk out of restaurants or shops if there's even just a short queue?

   • Why are we so often so busy?

⊡ investigate

☑ God's rest

In our modern world, lots of people are (rushing) around, living life in the fast lane. But in the Bible, (rest) is a really important theme.

In Genesis 1, on the seventh day of creation God rested from His work. This day is different to the other six—it doesn't end! The seventh day is the goal of creation—God enjoying perfect relationship with His creation. This is what we were made for. The seventh day—rest—is another way of speaking of enjoying life in God's kingdom.

▶ Read Hebrews 3 v 7 – 4 v 11

2. What was the "rest" these people failed to enter, do you think? Why didn't they get there?

> *Promised land i.e. return to Eden & life with God.*
>
> *Unbelief*

3. The promise of entering God's rest still remains for us today (4 v 1, 9). What is the rest to which we are heading? (See Revelation 14 v 13; 21 v 1-4 if you're stuck!)

> *Gods people, Place, rule, Presence,*

- Why is this exciting?

> *We only know creation marked, we any see so in a glass darkly*

4. How do we enter that promised rest (3 v 19 – 4 v 3)?

Faith in Christ

5. What lesson should we learn from what happened to "that generation" (3 v 12-14; 4 v 1-3, 11)?

Keep going! Keep the faith

⤷ apply

6. How can we make sure that we and our fellow believers do make it to the promised rest (3 v 12-13; 4 v 11)?

Look out for sin which entangles & ensures & lobs us of faith & rest

• In what practical ways do you, or could you, give this and receive this?

Send notes & messages

⊡ getting personal

How does the effort you put into making sure you enter God's eternal rest compare to the effort you put into other things (eg: your job, your hobbies)?

How much is your identity tied to the job you do? Do you think of yourself more as a worker ("I'm a teacher / cleaner / mother") or as a Christian, made for relationship with God?

What difference would it make to you if you saw yourself first and foremost as God's child, and your top priority was to enjoy knowing Him now and experiencing His rest eternally?

⬇ investigate

☑ Our rest

▶ Read Exodus 20 v 8-11; Deuteronomy 5 v 12-15

7. Why did God command His Old Testament people to take a day off each week?

• Exodus 20 v 11:

    To image Him,
    to bless them.

• Deuteronomy 5 v 12-15:

    Celebrate Gods rescue — they were there because
    of His work, not their
    own

• Exodus 23 v 12:

➡ apply

8. Bible-believing Christians differ over whether or not there is still a special weekly Sabbath day. Whatever our views on this issue, what principles can we draw from what we've learned above?

    1) we need physical & mental rest 2) we image
    God
    3) we celebrate His work

Are you taking enough time off for rest? Do you feel guilty when you take time off? If so, why?

Do you have a good balance of work and rest each day/week/year? Are you taking proper days off and holidays? Are you getting enough sleep? If not, what practical steps can you take?

⊡ investigate

The New Testament perspective on rest picks up similar ideas. At the most basic level, we need rest in our lives because we get tired (John 4 v 6; Mark 6 v 31)!

9. **Read Luke 10 v 38-42.** What did Martha need to learn about work and rest? How can we be like Martha?

    • How can we do today what Mary did then?

10. **Read Hebrews 10 v 24-25.** What else do we need time off work to do?

⊡ apply

11. In what ways will we (and those around us) suffer if we don't take seriously the need for time off work?

• What wrong views of your life will stop you resting regularly and properly?

• What motivations to rest have the passages we've looked at given you?

⊡ explore more

optional

▶ **Read Hebrews 3 v 13**

When do we need to encourage one another as believers? How could you do this?

⬆ pray

Spend some time **praising God** for the eternal rest He has prepared for you, and for showing you your need for regular rest now.

Then turn to **ask God** to help you have a right attitude to your work, so that you can rest obediently and trustingly. Ask Him to show you how you can encourage and challenge other believers to keep going in their faith.

5 Proverbs 31
WISDOM AT WORK

The story so far

Work is part of God's good plan for us and His world; but it has been spoiled by sin and judgment, so now is sometimes painful, futile, and unfair.

We are saved *by* Christ's work in His death and resurrection, not our own work. We are saved *for* working for God, doing good and building His church.

We must keep going in our faith so we can enjoy God's eternal rest; we remember that rest by resting from our work now.

⊕ talkabout

1. In India today there are 4 or 5 million "sadhus" living in caves, forests and temples. These sadhus are the ultra-committed holy men of Hinduism, who have withdrawn from the business of ordinary life. Through yoga, meditation and contemplation of God, they hope to achieve liberation from the cycle of reincarnation. What do you make of this?

⬇ investigate

☑ The foolish man at work

▶ **Read Proverbs 31 v 1-9**

The sense of verse 2 is: "What *are* you doing?"—three times. King Lemuel's mother is giving him a (literal) royal telling-off for being a fool at work!

> **DICTIONARY**
>
> **Inspired utterance (v 1):** a saying.

2. What three things did this king seem to have a problem with?

⊡ **explore more**

optional

> **Read Isaiah 11 v 1-5**

How is the coming King of this prophecy everything King Lemuel once wasn't, and everything we often fail to be too?

These words are fulfilled in Christ Jesus. How does Jesus being this kind of King encourage us:
* *when we see our own sinfulness?*
* *when we see our leaders' shortcomings?*

⊟ **apply**

3. In what ways are the misuse of sex, drink, and power temptations for us in our working lives?

⊡ **getting personal**

If King Lemuel's mum knew what you were up to at work, would she say to you: "What *are* you doing?" when it comes to:
* Sex: how do you relate to colleagues of the opposite sex? Do you flirt, or lust? Do you use pornography as an escape from the pressures of work?
* Drink: do you drink to cope with the stress of work? Do you have too much on the work-night-out?
* Power: are you using power at work to manipulate others and feed your own ego? Or are you using it to serve others and do good?

Where we're being fools, we need to turn from our sin, and ask God for forgiveness and wisdom. Do you need to do this now?

⊕ investigate

☑ The wise woman at work

The verses we're looking at next are a poem in which each verse begins with successive letters of the Hebrew alphabet. This A–Z structure is making the point that this woman covers all the bases. Proverbs is a style of biblical writing called "wisdom literature", which sees the world in black and white. This woman is the ideal, setting a standard no one can achieve this side of the new creation—in a sense, she's too good to be true! But there are important lessons we can learn from this ideal portrait.

▶ Read Proverbs 31 v 10-31

4. This wise woman's working life is described in verses 13-27. Make a list of her various activities.

buying, selling, working
making, providing,
caring, teaching

• Although her work is centred on the home, in what ways is she a bit more than what we tend to think of as a "housewife"?

A to Z of a woman.
Small business owner?

5. What is driving all this activity (v 30; see also 1 v 7)? What do you think this means and doesn't mean?

Seeing the world for what it really is and our place in it.

6. **Read Proverbs 6 v 6-11 and ~~26 v 13-16.~~** How does this "fool" compare to the wise woman of chapter 31?

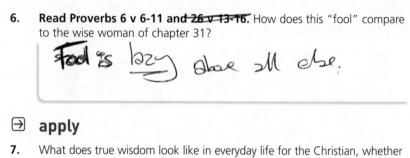

Fool is lazy above all else.

→ **apply**

7. What does true wisdom look like in everyday life for the Christian, whether man or woman? How ~~does true wisdom look different from the "Hindu sadhu"?~~

Live at our position with God in mind.
Seek to honour Him in all thys.

8. Most of our "heroes of the faith" in church history tend to be people who have been in full-time gospel work as missionaries or church ministers or theologians. How does this passage challenge that?

9. Sarah spends her days at home, looking after her three kids. She trained as a lawyer and has been at home now for six years. Sometimes friends who go out to work say things like: "What do you get up to all day?" and "Are you going to go back to work at some point?" It's getting annoying and it's getting her down!

How could you encourage her from this passage? And if you were her husband, how would verses 28-31 challenge you?

⊡ getting personal

Do you ever feel that God is only interested in the few minutes a day you spend reading the Bible and praying? God delights in our serving Him in the other 95% of our day as well. Give thanks to God for that now, and let it change your attitude tomorrow!

Sometimes, we can be hardworking in some areas of life but lazy in others. For example, a Christian man may work hard in his job, but be lazy when it comes to caring for his wife and leading his family, or serving at church, or growing spiritually. In which areas of life might you be guilty of this? How do you need to change?

⊡ investigate

In Proverbs 9, we meet two women who aren't real women at all, but who picture the basic choice we face in life—between wisdom and folly. When you compare 31 v 10 with 3 v 13-15, the ideal woman in chapter 31 is at one level "Lady Wisdom" making a final appearance and urging us to choose her in life.

❯ Read Colossians 2 v 3

10. What will this wise choice look like for us, living in the twenty-first century rather than in Old Testament Israel?

Where then is real wisdom?
❋ In Christ

⊡ apply

11. "In God's sight, wisdom is more important than intelligence." What do you make of this statement? What are its implications?

See pg 74

⬆ pray

Thank God:

- for Jesus, whose perfect, wise life given for us has paid for all our sins.
- that He is interested in all of our life, including our work, not just our times of prayer and Bible reading.

Ask God:

- for a right fear of Him, and the commitment to living that out each day in practical godliness.
- for forgiveness for ways in which we are fools in our working life, and for power by His Spirit to live wisely.
- for those wanting to get married to choose a husband or wife wisely.

6 WITNESS AT WORK

Colossians 3 v 22 – 4 v 6

The story so far

We are saved *by* Christ's work in His death and resurrection, not our own work. We are saved *for* working for God, doing good and building His church.

We must keep going in our faith so we can enjoy God's eternal rest; we remember that rest by resting from our work now.

We should live wisely at work, with a right respect for God, and beware the pitfalls of sex, drink and power.

⊕ talkabout

1. "Preach the gospel. Use words if necessary." What do you agree and/or disagree with in this statement?

⊕ investigate

❯ Read Colossians 3 v 22 – 4 v 1

In this passage, the apostle Paul is giving instructions to Christian slaves and masters. In the first-century world, slavery was very widespread. In Italy, a third of the population were slaves, working in business and shops, as cooks and cleaners, teachers and doctors, in mines and on farms. In some (though by no means all) respects, being a slave back then wasn't so different from working life today; and so we can apply this teaching to the workplace.

> **DICTIONARY**
>
> **Inheritance (3 v 24):** a place in God's eternal kingdom (1 v 12).

2. How should the Christian behave at work? How do you think this behaviour might contrast with how others behave at work?

3. Which phrases refer to the motivation for behaving this way at work?

4. If someone is in a job where they have people working for them, how should they behave?

⤷ **apply**

5. It's easy to forget about the Lord in the busyness of work. What can we do to help us keep Him at the centre of all we do during a working day?

6. We are not being told to be workaholics or perfectionists! What difference is there between godliness and workaholism? How do you tell which you are, do you think?

7. Share any encouraging stories of people noticing that Christians are different at work, either from your own experience or that of others you know.

⊡ getting personal

Which of these commands do you find hardest to obey? Why? What truths do you need to remember to help you joyfully obey?

⊡ explore more

optional

▶ **Read Titus 2 v 9-10**

What motivation is given here for godly behaviour at work? What does that mean?

▶ **Read Matthew 5 v 16**

How is Titus 2 confirming what Jesus teaches here?
Why do people need to know we are Christian, as well as seeing us behave as Christians?

⊡ investigate

These next few verses are no longer specifically for slaves and masters; but we can still apply the principles to our workplaces.

▶ **Read Colossians 4 v 2-6**

8. What two things did Paul ask for prayer about?

> **DICTIONARY**
>
> **Mystery (v 3):**
> something hidden which has now been revealed (see 1 v 25-27).

• Why do you think we too need to pray this?

9. What does verse 5 say about people, and about time? How does this help us in sharing the gospel at work?

10. The phrase "know how to answer" (v 6) implies that people will ask questions. What do you think might prompt people to do that?

⊟ apply

11. The phrase "for which I am in chains" reminds us that sharing the gospel is a costly business. What do you think that cost might look like for you, in your workplace?

12. This passage has taught us both to live out the gospel life and pass on the gospel message. What would happen if we did the first, but not the second?

• What would happen if we did the second, but not the first?

⊡ getting personal

Do people at work know you are Christian? If not, pray for courage to speak out.

Does your behaviour at work advertise or undermine the gospel? What behaviour or attitude do you most need to work on?

Are there other Christians in your workplace? How could you encourage one another in living for Christ and getting the gospel out in that place?

↑ pray

Thank God:

• that He notices everything you do at work, even when others don't.

• for putting people who don't know Jesus alongside you in your workplace, so they can see the gospel in you.

• for the opportunities you get to show and share the gospel message.

Ask God:

• to motivate you in your work with the knowledge that you're working for Him.

• for courage to live as a Christian and speak as a Christian, despite the cost.

• to give you an opportunity to speak to specific co-workers this week. (You could write their names down here, and pray for each other and for them during the week.)

7 1 Timothy 6 v 6-10, 17-19
MONEY AND WORK

The story so far

Having been saved by God's work in Christ, we must keep going so we can enjoy God's eternal rest; we remember that rest by resting from our work now.

We should live wisely at work, with a right respect for God, and beware the pitfalls of sex, drink and power.

Whatever we're doing in our work, we can and should do it for God, who sees it all; and we can and should be telling those around us about His Son.

⊕ talkabout

1. What is the connection between work and money?

⊕ investigate

> ❯ Read 1 Timothy 6 v 6-10

2. What attitude do verses 6-8 urge us to have? Why?

DICTIONARY

Contentment (v 6): being satisfied with what you have.
Clothing (v 8): literally "covering"—so could include a roof over your head, as well as clothes on your body.

3. How is the desire to get rich harmful (v 9-10)? What might this look like in 21st-century life?

4. "The love of money is a root of all kinds of evil" (v 10) is sometimes misquoted as "money is the root of all evil". There are three differences. What are they? Why are they important?

5. **Read Matthew 6 v 24.** How do Paul's words to Timothy echo Jesus' warning here?

⮕ apply

6. How does advertising fuel the love of money, and rob us of contentment?

7. Why do we try to serve God and money?

8. What might be some signs that we do love money? What action should we take if we do?

• How would you want others to react if they noticed it in you?

⊡ **explore more**

optional

▶ **Read Luke 16 v 14-15**

What is surprising here?

▶ **Read 2 Thessalonians 3 v 7-12**

How should we treat someone who refuses to work to provide for themselves? What if someone is unable to work or to find work?

⬇ investigate

❯ Read 1 Timothy 6 v 17-19

9. For those who are rich, what are:
• the dangers?

• the duties?

• incentives for performing those duties?

➔ apply

10. Imagine that someone at church says to you: "I don't have a problem
with money. I give 10% of my income to the church." How would you
respond?

⊡ getting personal

Do you give thanks each day to God, "who richly provides us with
everything for our enjoyment"? Would it help you to set a particular
time in the day when you do this?

Do you think you should be more generous? What is stopping you
from giving more? How will you avoid giving grudgingly?

⬆ pray

Thank God:

- for this warning about the dangers of loving money.
- for His generosity in giving you good gifts to enjoy.
- for any means He's currently blessing you with which enable you to support yourself (and your family).

Ask God:

- to make you truly content in Christ, and not in love with money.
- to enable you to be joyfully generous with your money and possessions.
- to help you with any particular changes this study has challenged you to make.

8
Matthew 6 v 25-34
WORRY AT WORK

The story so far

We should live wisely at work, with a right respect for God, and beware the pitfalls of sex, drink and power.

Whatever we're doing in our work, we can and should do it for God, who sees it all; and we can and should be telling those around us about His Son.

Our contentment should come from knowing Jesus, not having money—and so we can be generous with all the money and possessions He has given us.

⊕ talkabout

1. What kind of work things do people worry about?

• In what different ways does work-related worry affect people?

⊕ investigate

▶ Read Matthew 6 v 25-34

This passage isn't specifically about work, but in it Jesus gives us three remedies for worry which can help set us free from our work worries!

DICTIONARY

Pagans (v 32): non-Christians.
Kingdom (v 33): God's rule through King Jesus.
Righteousness (v 33): here, it means living a godly life, which reflects God's character.

2. What reason does Jesus give for not worrying in verse 25? What does He mean?

3. What do the birds and flowers teach us (v 26, v 28-30)? How does Jesus' description of His disciples in verse 30 show they needed this lesson?

⤷ apply

4. Mike is a school teacher who is constantly worried about work. He worries about whether or not his pupils like him; whether his classes will get good results; how he compares to other teachers; whether his lessons are good enough; whether he'll get promoted…
How could you use this truth of our heavenly Father's care to comfort him?

Remedy One =

⊡ explore more

optional

> **▶ Read Philippians 4 v 6-7**

What are we to do with our worries? What assurance is given to encourage us to do this? What things keep us from doing this more?

⊥ **investigate**

5. In verses 27 and 34, Jesus gives two reasons why there is no point in worrying. What are they?

➔ **apply**

6. The future is *not* in our hands; it *is* in God's. How does knowing these are both true help us?

7. In what sense are we to live "one day at a time"? Where does that leave planning for the future, do you think?

Remedy Two =

⊡ explore more

> **Read Matthew 10 v 29-30**

What does Jesus teach about God's control over our lives?

> **Read Philippians 2 v 20; 4 v 6**

In the original Greek, "genuine concern" and "anxious" are the same word. So what would you say is the difference between a right concern, and a wrong worry?

⊌ investigate

8. What does Jesus say non-Christians run after (v 31-33)? Why does He choose the phrase "run after", do you think?

9. In what way should the priorities of Jesus' followers be different? What does that mean?

⊟ apply

10. How do advertisements and the titles of glossy magazines show that the things people chase after has not changed much since the first century?

11. What might it look like to "seek first his kingdom" in your workplaces?

Remedy Three =

🔅 getting personal

Write down one work-related (or other) worry you have at the moment. Which of the truths you've learned today will help you most in dealing with it?

Sometimes our pride keeps us from telling other believers about our worries. But they can only support us and pray for us (and with us) if they know what our struggles are. Who can you be honest with about your worries?

12. Think over what we've seen the Bible says about work. What changes to your attitude or actions are you prompted to make?

⬆ pray

Thank God:

- that His Fatherly care, sovereign control, and eternal kingdom mean we have no need to worry.
- that His perfect word excites us about work, equips us to deal with work, and shows us how to live for Him at work.

Ask God:

- for help to trust Him instead of worrying, and to encourage and challenge each other in this. You might want to mention specific concerns as you pray.

Making work work: Leader's Guide

INTRODUCTION

Leading a Bible study can be a bit like herding cats—everyone has a different idea of what the passage could be about, and a different line of enquiry that they want to pursue. But a good group leader is more than someone who just referees this kind of discussion. You will want to:

- correctly understand and handle the Bible passage. But also…

- encourage and train the people in your group to do this for themselves. Don't fall into the trap of spoon-feeding people by simply passing on the information in the Leader's Guide. Then…

- make sure that no Bible study is finished without everyone knowing how the passage is relevant for them. What changes do you all need to make in the light of the things you have been learning? And finally…

- encourage the group to turn all that has been learned and discussed into prayer.

Your Bible-study group is unique, and you are likely to know better than anyone the capabilities, backgrounds and circumstances of the people you are leading. That's why we've designed these guides with a number of optional features. If they're a quiet bunch, you might want to spend longer on talkabout. If your time is limited, you can choose to skip explore more, or get people to look at these questions at home. Can't get enough of Bible study? Well, some studies have optional extra homework projects. As leader, you can adapt and select the material to the needs of your particular group.

So what's in the Leader's Guide? The main thing that this Leader's Guide will help you to do is to understand the major teaching points in the passage you are studying, and how to apply them. As well as guidance on the questions, the Leader's Guide for each session contains the following important sections:

THE BIG IDEA

One or two key sentences will give you the main point of the session. This is what you should be aiming to have fixed in people's minds as they leave the Bible study. And it's the point you need to head back towards when the discussion goes off at a tangent.

SUMMARY

An overview of the passage, including plenty of useful historical background information.

OPTIONAL EXTRA

Usually this is an introductory activity that ties in with the main theme of the Bible study, and is designed to "break the ice" at the beginning of a session. Or it may be a "homework project" that people can tackle during the week.

So let's take a look at the various different features of a Good Book Guide:

⊕ talkabout

Each session kicks off with a discussion question, based on the group's opinions or experiences. It's designed to get people talking and thinking in a general way about the main subject of the Bible study.

⬇ investigate

The first thing you and your group need to know is what the Bible passage is about, which is the purpose of these questions. But watch out—people may come up with answers based on their experiences or teaching they have heard in the past, without referring to the passage at all. It's amazing how often we can get through a Bible study without actually looking at the Bible! If you're stuck for an answer, the Leader's Guide contains guidance on questions. These are the answers to direct your group to. This information isn't meant to be read out to people—ideally, you want them to discover these answers from the Bible for themselves. Sometimes there are optional follow-up questions (see ☑ in guidance on questions) to help you help your group get to the answer.

⬇ explore more

These questions generally point people to other relevant parts of the Bible. They are useful for helping your group to see how the passage fits into the "big picture" of the whole Bible. These sections are OPTIONAL—only use them if you have time. Remember that it's better to finish in good time having really grasped one big thing from the passage, than to try and cram everything in.

➡ apply

We want to encourage you to spend more time working at application—too often, it is simply tacked on at the end. In the Good Book Guides, apply sections are mixed in with the investigate sections of the study. We hope that people will realise that application is not just an optional extra, but rather, the whole purpose of studying the

Bible. We do Bible study so that our lives can be changed by what we hear from God's word. If you skip the application, the Bible study hasn't achieved its purpose.

These questions draw out practical lessons that we can all learn from the Bible passage. You can review what has been learned so far, and think about practical differences that this should make in our churches and our lives. The group gets the opportunity to talk about what they personally have learned.

⬇ getting personal

These can be done at home, but it is well worth allowing a few moments of quiet reflection during the study for each person to think and pray about specific changes they need to make in their own lives. Why not have a time for reporting back at the beginning of the following session, so that everyone can be encouraged and challenged by one another to make application a priority?

⬆ pray

In Acts 4 v 25-30 the first Christians quoted Psalm 2 as they prayed in response to the persecution of the apostles by the Jewish religious leaders. Today however, it's not as common for Christians to base prayers on the truths of God's word as it once was. As a result, our prayers tend to be weak, superficial and self-centred rather than bold, visionary and God-centred.

The prayer section is based on what has been learned from the Bible passage. How different our prayer times would be if we were genuinely responding to what God has said to us through His word.

1 Genesis 1 v 26 – 2 v 25
PURPOSE AT WORK

THE BIG IDEA
Our daily work, inside or outside the home, is part of God's good design for us, ruling the world under Him.

SUMMARY
This opening study is foundational for understanding the place of daily work in God's plans and purposes. The first two chapters of Genesis reveal that God, the loving Creator and Ruler of everything, made us to rule the world under His authority.

For Adam, this rule included a specific job of looking after the Garden of Eden. And so for each of us, our daily work is part of how we are to serve the Lord in ruling the world under Him. Work is not a curse! It was part of God's good design for our world.

To help Adam in his God-given task, God gave him the gift of a wife and children. So work involves not just the "work of the garden" but also the "work of the home" (marriage and family). It is important for the rest of the studies (and for how we view ourselves and our lives) that we don't think of "work" only in terms of what happens in the office/factory, but also of how we labour in the home. There is great God-given value in being a stay-at-home parent.

OPTIONAL EXTRA
Here are two games you could play in order to get people thinking about how varied work is:
- *Job charades:* Split the group into two teams. Give each team 20 bits of paper in a bag with a different job written on each (eg: teacher, plumber, doctor, pilot, shop assistant). The team members take it in turns to take out a bit of paper and act out the job to the group. When the team guesses correctly, it's the next person's turn. The team that finishes first wins.
- *Job brainstorming:* Split the group into pairs and give them 3 minutes to write down as many different jobs as they can think of. The pair with the most at the end wins.

GUIDANCE FOR QUESTIONS
1. How would you define work? At the most basic level, work is the job you do. It may be paid or unpaid, full-time or part-time. Some go out to work, whereas for others their work is staying at home looking after the kids. And then there is the gospel work which all Christians should be doing in building God's church (which we'll look at more in Study Three). Someone may be retired from their job or "out of work" but still hard at work in lots of other ways! Allow your group to discuss this question; they don't need to reach the "right answer"—you could return to the question at the end of the study to see if the group want to add to, or amend, their answer.

- **What is the point of work?** There are various possible answers, including:
  - Never really think about it.
  - Work is a necessary evil. I work to earn money to pay the bills and go on holiday. I live for the weekend.
  - Work is an opportunity to get to know non-Christians so I can evangelise them.
  - Work is one way I serve the Lord.

2. What task does God give mankind to do? What do you think that means? To have dominion and rule over the earth. God is the Creator and loving Ruler of the world, and part of being made in His image is that we are to rule the world with Him, under His authority. This rule is not to be harsh or oppressive but to mirror the loving care which God exercises over the world.

3. What particular job does God give Adam to do? How is this part of his God-given task? To work and care for the garden. God created Adam for this grand purpose of ruling over all the earth, but when he got up on Monday morning that meant going to work in the garden where God had put him. This work is only part of ruling the world under God
Note: This is only *part* of the job—there is more to ruling than work. Ruling the world also meant obeying God's command not to eat from the tree of knowledge of good and evil. Adam was to resist the devil and express his rule in that way, too.

4. How do God's work and man's work go together in v 5, 8, 15? God planted the garden and watered it with rain, but it needed man to work it. God set things up as a partnership, making man's work a vital link in the chain. In that first garden we see on a small scale how the world was to function, and the place and importance of our work. God the Creator and loving Ruler does His work of providing the natural resources and raw materials, and sustaining life and making things grow. His people, ruling under Him, do their work as developers and cultivators. Both God's work and human work are necessary, and go hand in hand.

5. APPLY: Jesus told us to pray: "Give us each day our daily bread" (Luke 11

v 3); but how do God's work and human work need to come together before we find a loaf of bread in our kitchen??** God gives us our daily bread, but there would be nothing to butter in your kitchen if it wasn't for the hard work of the farmer, the baker, the truck-driver and the team at your local supermarket.

6. APPLY: Work is part of God's flawless, original creation. How should this shape our attitude to our work? That God has set things up to function like this, and that work is given by God before sin entered the world (in Genesis 3) tells us that work is a good thing—a blessing, not a curse! Part of what it means to be human is to work. God wants us to enjoy our work (Ecclesiastes 3 v 22) and to do it to serve Him (Colossians 3 v 23-24).

• **How does it help us understand why being unemployed can be so hard?** One reason unemployment can be so hard is that you may feel you're not making any contribution but just being a drain on society. One young guy who'd been out of work for 5 years since leaving school was interviewed on the radio. He'd just been given an apprenticeship doing plastering and joinery on a housing project and said: "I feel like I'm doing something and playing a role in the world now". This is part of what we were created to do.

7. APPLY: Put the following jobs in order of importance: car mechanic, missionary, refuse collector, doctor, shop assistant, banker, teacher, church leader, brain surgeon. To make the exercise easier you could write the jobs on bits of paper and get people in twos or threes to put them in order. Often people have a list with missionary at the top and refuse collector at the bottom. But all work is good. As long as a job isn't illegal or immoral (eg: assassin, prostitute, pimp, thief—see Ephesians 4 v 28), any job is good and can be done to serve God.

- **As Christians, does it matter what job we do?** No! What matters is not what we do, so much as how we do it—our attitude and diligence, etc. Of course, there is nothing wrong with hoping for and seeking a job in which we'll feel fulfilled, which uses our gifts and abilities, and so on. But ultimately, no one job is intrinsically more worthy than another. Often, we put full-time paid gospel work on a pedestal; the rest of us "just" do secular work, and don't serve the Lord full-time. But *all* jobs can be used to serve the Lord, because they're part of our God-given task of "ruling".

EXPLORE MORE

"Christians working in banking or the Armed Forces should do something more worthwhile instead, such as becoming doctors or teachers." What [does Luke 3 v 12-14] say to this idea? We mustn't put caring professions on a pedestal—doctors and nurses and teachers. When taxmen and soldiers came to John the Baptist, he didn't tell them to leave their jobs and do something more worthwhile. He told them to go back and be godly tax collectors and godly soldiers.

Some people look down on those who do manual work (eg: builders or mechanics). What does [Mark 6 v 3] say to that? When God became flesh, He spent a large part of His working life as a carpenter, doing manual labour. If we look down on people because of the job they do, we are not thinking like God. Whether we work with our head or hands,

or both, doesn't matter. And if all the refuse collectors stopped work tomorrow, it would affect our lives as much as (or more than) if the brain-surgeons went on strike!

Imagine a Christian teenager asks you how they should decide what job to do. What advice would you give them? A good question to ask is: "How can I best serve God in His world as the person I am, with the gifts and skills and opportunities that God has given me?" If you have a choice of job (which many in the world today don't, so that's something to be thankful for), it's not wrong to choose something you would enjoy doing.

8. What does God say [in Gen 2 v 18-25] is not good? How does He solve the problem? In 1 v 31, God declared everything He had made was good. But now, God sees that it isn't good for the man to be alone and he needs a helper in this task of ruling the world (2 v 18). And so He creates woman (v 21-22). The problem isn't only being lonely and needing companionship, but being alone in the task and needing help. The man delights in the woman (v 23) and God brings them together in marriage (v 24-25). Marriage involves leaving, joining, and becoming one flesh.

9. What does 1 v 28 suggest is one purpose of marriage? How does this help humanity "rule over" the earth?! In v 28 "filling the earth" is linked with ruling over it. If Adam was to fulfil his God-given task of ruling the world, more "gardeners" were needed. One of the purposes of marriage is to produce children who will be able to work in God's world. This means that having, and raising, children, is just as much a part of our God-given work of "ruling" as going "gardening" is.

10. APPLY: What do people in our society think of the work of bearing children, raising a family and running a home compared to "pursuing a career"? How similar or different is this to God's view? Many mothers are made to feel: "I'm only a mother", and are looked down on as someone who doesn't work. People think disdainfully: "What do they do all day?" or ask: "When are you going to go back to work?" And some parents sacrifice the welfare of their children for the sake of career, or make the mistake of thinking that their children need lots of gifts, or an expensive education, or a large house, etc, more than they need to have time with both their father and mother. But in God's good design, the hard work of bearing and raising children is every bit as important as other types of work. There's more to life than the work of "the garden"—there's the work of "the home". No one says at the end of their life: "I wish I'd spent more time at the office"!

11. APPLY: How might we use our work as an excuse for neglecting our marriage (or vice versa)? By being "married to the job" and investing all our time and energy in that, while perhaps justifying it as being for the sake of our spouse and children. By spending longer at work than we need to in order to avoid having to deal with issues at home. If we are married, we mustn't just devote ourselves to "cultivating the garden" in our jobs, but also to cultivating our marriages. God wants us to invest time and energy and commitment in that relationship. At the other extreme, there are those who do the bare minimum at work because family is all-important; or use work time to call their wife/husband; or never focus on their job because they are thinking about their family.

12. APPLY: Sum up what we've learned about the ultimate point of work. What is the key truth you will take away from this study? The ultimate point of our work is to serve the Lord, our work being one way in which we rule the world under His authority. You might like to tell the group a story about three stone-masons in a medieval stone-mason's yard. A visitor asked each of them what they were doing. The first said: "I'm cutting a stone". The second answered: "I'm earning my living". But the third held his head high and said: "I'm building a cathedral". The visitor commented about the third one that: "He looked beyond his tools and his wages to the ultimate end he was serving". That is a biblical perspective on work—but we can lift our eyes from our task and our wage not to cathedral-building, but to our part in God's purpose for us as humans, of ruling the world under Him and enjoying our role in His world.

2 Genesis 3; 4; 11; 31
TROUBLE AT WORK

THE BIG IDEA
In a fallen world, work has been spoiled by pain, futility, broken relationships, godless ambition, and unfair treatment.

SUMMARY
From the first study we might expect that work would be pure joy, ruling the world under God's authority and serving Him in our work with delight and fulfilment. But now, since the fall, we live in a world suffering the effects of sin and God's judgment, and this means that our experience of work is going to be bitter-sweet. God's good design in Genesis 1 – 2 is not ripped up and thrown away, but it is messed up and distorted.

As Christians, we are still to serve God in the work of the garden and the work of the home, and we may still find joy and satisfaction in that, but there will also be pain and difficulty. Seeing this can free us from the added burden of guilt, thinking: "I shouldn't be finding things so hard". For those struggling at the moment with how hard working life is, it may come as huge relief to realise that this is not a sign of being spiritually unfaithful or immature. Work is hard. We need to look to God for help and to one another for support.

We'll look at five examples in Genesis of how sin and judgment affect work.
• Work now involves painful toil.
• It is overshadowed by death.
• Relationships at work go wrong because of the sins in our hearts.
• There is godless ambition.
• People suffer from unfair conditions.

OPTIONAL EXTRA
Game: ask group members to write down on a piece of paper what their dream job would be. Fold them and put them in a bag. Then take it in turns to go round taking out a piece of paper and guessing who you think wrote it. Once each person has had a turn, get the group members to reveal which was theirs. Hopefully by the end of the study it will be clear that actually even our dream job would be hard-going, because in a fallen world no job is free from the effects of sin and judgment.

GUIDANCE FOR QUESTIONS
1. Share any holiday experiences you have had (or heard about) when the reality didn't live up to what you'd expected from the brochure. For example, a woman booked a dream holiday in Spain. The brochure pictures were amazing; a beautiful apartment overlooking the sea in a quiet village. But when she got there, she found a building site next-door, and she spent her holiday on the phone every day, complaining about the noise of hammering and trying to negotiate compensation. In addition it turned out that the people next door were smokers, and the apartment balconies were so close together that these neighbours could see into their apartment when they were out smoking on their balcony. The reality was a far cry from the images in the glossy brochure. You could bring in some holiday brochures and imagine what might be just out of the camera frame!

• **In what ways does your experience of work not always (or ever!) match that glossy brochure?** This is a chance for the group to start to think about what is hard in their experience of work. If as the leader you share something you find hard at work (whether in the factory/office or the home), that will help others to be honest about their own struggles.

2. In what ways did the "work of the home" become painful for the woman? When God judged the man and the woman for their rebellion, their areas of work were directly affected. In the "work of the home", bringing children into the world would now be painful, as would bringing them up—not just a delight, but also exhausting, discouraging, and full of heartache as sometimes children don't turn out as you would want. Think of the heartache Cain & Abel caused their parents! And the whole project of cultivating a marriage would become hard because it now involved two sinners. The woman would now seek to rule over the husband. ("Desire" in v 16 is a desire to dominate; the same word is used in 4 v 7 about sin's desire to control Cain.)

- **In what ways did the "work of the garden" become painful for the man?** The man's job was to work in the garden, but now the ground is cursed, thorns and thistles grow, and work becomes sweat and toil. Adam would no longer have just leapt out of bed on a Monday morning saying: "Yippee, another week at work!" Working life now has plenty of frustrations, things do go wrong, and the pressures may at times feel overwhelming.

3. Part of God's judgment on mankind was death. What impact does knowing we will die one day have on how we see our work day by day? Our work can seem so meaningless in the face of death. It can seem so important at the time, and we get so stressed out about it, but does it ultimately matter? When one day you're facing death, how important will any of it seem then? The reality of death will affect our work, even as Christians, because we too are living and working in a creation that has now been subjected to futility and bondage to decay.

4. Why did Cain kill his brother? Because he was angry and envious. The corruption in his heart was expressed in his relationships—in the workplace (ie: the field).

5. APPLY: How do things like anger, envy, and hatred reveal themselves in your workplaces? For some, the hardest thing about work is not so much the work itself but relationships at work. Sin, as it is expressed in relationships, can be a big source of stress at work. The gossip, slander, rivalry, envy, selfishness, egos, unkindness, harassment. The "politics", which is about people manipulating others to get what they want. And sometimes there can be a particular relationship at work which causes you no end of grief. There may be someone who seems to have it in for you, or whom you don't get on with, and whom you dread meeting. As Christians, these things will affect us because this is the world in which we work. And we will see these things in our hearts as well, but we are to be different. Our godliness at work should make us stand out. The people we are at work and the way we relate at work are supremely important. They matter even more than the actual work we do.

6. What was these people's ambition in building this tower (11 v 4)? They wanted to make a name for themselves, instead of being concerned with God's name. And the ambition to build a tower with its top in the heavens suggests the desire not to get to God, but rather to replace God. The sense is: "We will ascend to the heavens. We will be god".

• **What was wrong about this (look back at 1 v 26-28)?** They were supposed to be ruling the world under God and for Him, not without and in rejection of Him. Part of their ruling under God was to fill the earth; but now they are building a city and tower so that they won't "be scattered over the face of the whole earth" (11 v 4).

7. APPLY: How do people seek to make a reputation for themselves through work today? Working for their own glory and reputation and promotion. People not working to serve God or others, but to serve themselves. Doing whatever it takes to get to the top. Prepared to sacrifice anything (family, principles) in their desire for power and recognition and money. Driven by the ambition to make their tower bigger than the next person's. Ecclesiastes 4 v 4 says: "I saw that all toil and all achievement spring from man's envy of his neighbour".

• **What adverse effects of this "tower-building" have you seen?** It creates rivalry. And once we leave God out, the "tower-building project" becomes a new centre of life. Instead of living for God, people live for work and that becomes the centre of life, where they look for meaning and purpose and worth. Such godless ambition in the workplace can make it a difficult place for the Christian. If people have made work the centre of life, replacing God, then they will have different priorities from the Christian. They won't understand when a Christian says: "I'm not living for work. I'm living for God. And so I've got other things in life which are important—church, spouse, family."

It is not only our own tower-building, but also the tower-building of others, which makes it harder to live as a Christian.

8. In what ways was Jacob's working life unfair? What kept him going? Not only were his working conditions hard—sweltering in the day, freezing at night—but he was repeatedly cheated by his employer, who kept changing his wages. And this had been going on for 20 years. Jacob kept going because he trusted in the Lord and knew that He was with him.

9. APPLY: Can you relate at all to his experience? How did you (or were you tempted to) react? Working life in a fallen world can be very unfair. You may have an unfair boss who doesn't appreciate the work you do, who takes credit for it, who makes unreasonable demands on you. You may not get the recognition or promotion you deserve. You may not get paid as much as you should. You may lose your job in spite of having worked well. In such situations we can be tempted to blame God instead of trusting in Him and knowing He is with us.

EXPLORE MORE
Read Genesis 39 v 6b-20. How was Joseph unfairly treated at work because he obeyed God? Joseph resisted the sexual advances of his boss's wife when she tried to seduce him. She hit back by falsely accusing him. He lost his job and wound up in prison. Obeying God carried a high price.
Read 1 Peter 2 v 18-23. How does the example of Christ encourage us when we are unfairly treated at work? Peter tells Christian slaves who were suffering for doing good under harsh masters that they should be encouraged by the example of Christ: "To this you were called, because Christ suffered for you" (v 21). It's not

wrong to go to our employer when we're being unfairly treated, but even more important that we go to God. Jesus didn't try to get even but instead "entrusted himself to him who judges justly" (v 23), and so should we (see also 4 v 19). If you are being unfairly treated at work, that can be a huge stress and burden to carry, but you are in good company with Jacob, Joseph, and Jesus. Don't become bitter and resentful. Do tell Christian friends so they can support you and pray for you.

⊻

• Joseph's descendants ended up working as slaves in Egypt (Exodus 1 v 12-14). They knew work as bitter oppression—and so do many today. What does Psalm 82 v 3-4 tell us should be our response? What would this look like for you, in your society?

10. APPLY: Look back over this whole study. Why do you think it's important to be realistic about the difficulties of working life in a fallen world? We need to understand not just what God's good design is but also how the fall has affected our work. Otherwise we're going to have unrealistic expectations of work and feel guilty that maybe we're doing something wrong because we're finding it hard-going. We won't feel able to be honest with fellow believers about our struggles, and so won't get the help and support we all need.

• **Which of the five aspects of work in a fallen world can you relate to most? Have you learned anything from these passages that will help you deal with them next time?** Different parts of the session will have struck people differently. This final question is a chance for group members to share what has been most relevant to them in their situation at the moment, so we can pray for one another.

3 Ephesians 2; 4
SAVIOUR AT WORK

THE BIG IDEA

We are saved *by* Christ's work in His death and resurrection, not by our own work. We are saved *for* working for Him, building His church.

SUMMARY

The purpose for which we were created, ruling the world under God, is now not just hard but impossible, humanly speaking.

Ephesians 2 tells us that far from ruling under God, our natural condition now is that we are spiritually dead, enslaved to

the world, the flesh and the devil, and under God's condemnation. If we are ever going to be restored to our position of rule under God, we need His work of salvation. God's work for us in history centred on Him sending His Son, Jesus, to die for us and to be raised to life. Through faith, we are united with Christ and are spiritually raised from death to life to rule with Him, living a life of good works. This places our own work (both moral "works" and what we do Monday to Friday) in perspective. None of our work can earn what we most need—new, eternal life. We have to look to another's work—to the Lord Jesus—for that.

God's purpose is not just to have individuals restored to rule under Him, but to have a people united together, who will one day rule with Him in the age to come. In the present age, the people of God are pictured as a temple which God is building, and as a body which is growing. God wants each of us to be fully devoted to this work of growing this building and body, what the Bible calls the "work of the Lord" (1 Cor 15 v 58). The body of Christ grows as we use our different gifts to serve one another, and as we reach out to the world with the gospel. This is what we're saved *for*.

OPTIONAL EXTRA

This study highlights the "impossible job" of saving ourselves. Get people in pairs to come up with three tasks they do reasonably regularly, and which they find impossible, and then share them with the group. Eg:

- growing lettuces that aren't nibbled by snails or slugs.
- doing the laundry and ending up with no odd socks
- doing DIY without having to buy any new equipment or screws.

GUIDANCE FOR QUESTIONS

1. If you did a street survey, what sort of answers would you get to the questions: • What is wrong with world? • What is the solution? Obviously, the answers to the second part of this question will be affected by the answers given to the first! But possibilities include:

- There are some bad people who are ruining things for everyone else – they need dealing with.
- The political and economic system is at fault and needs changing.

- The social conditions in which people are living make them behave badly, so their living standards need improving and they need better education.
- The problem is religion which causes divisions and wars—especially the fundamentalist ones which think they alone are right. We need to be rid of religion or get people to be more tolerant.

2. What is the spiritual condition of humanity (v 1-3)? Instead of enjoying life with God, we are spiritually dead (v 1) because of our sins. Instead of ruling we are ruled over by the world, the sinful nature, and the devil (v 2-3). And instead of rejoicing in our Creator, we are condemned by Him as our Judge (v 3).

- **Is this how people see themselves?** Most people have no idea how serious their condition is. They are physically alive and don't realise that they are spiritually dead. They think they are free to live as they want and don't realise that they are enslaved. They think that God, if He exists, must be quite pleased with them, and don't realise that He is angry with them.

3. What has God done for Christians (v 4-7)? Why has He done this? He has saved us (v 5). We were spiritually dead, but God has made us alive; we were enslaved, but God has seated us in a position of rule—a spiritual reality now but in the age to come we will rule with Him and God's creation purpose will be gloriously fulfilled; we were condemned, but now we are objects of God's rich mercy, great love and kindness. This transformation has come about through being united with Christ (v 5: "made us alive with Christ"; v 6: "raised us up with Christ and seated us with him"). It's all by God's grace, His undeserved love.

4. What do verses 8-10 emphasise about how we are saved; and about how we are *not* saved? We are saved by grace (God's undeserved kindness) through faith (us simply receiving His gift of life in Jesus). So salvation is the gift of God. We are God's workmanship, re-created by God. Salvation is *not* from ourselves—it is nothing to do with who we are or what we do. (Therefore, no one can boast—the thing we most need is the thing we cannot achieve ourselves.)

5. What place do good works have in the Christian life (v 10)? We are not saved *by* good works, but we are saved *for* good works. God has recreated us in Christ for this very purpose. Now we are no longer enslaved to the world, the sinful nature and the devil, but set free to live for God and to do the good works He has prepared for us. Notice that even the good works that we now do are a gift from God—He's prepared them ahead of time, for us to do.

6. APPLY: How does this passage show us the limits of our own work (in the home, the office, the factory, our church, or anywhere else)? We can never fulfil God's good creation purpose for us and get back to Genesis 1 – 2 by just working hard. We need God's work of salvation for us in Christ. Only then can our work become again a way of serving God in His world.

7. What is God's goal for the body? Growth—for the body to be built up (v 12) and grow to maturity (v 13, 15, 16). Perhaps we could include growth in numbers as well.

8. What do God's people have (v 7-8)? Grace. "Each"—every—Christian has been given grace, just as Jesus chose to give it (v 7). This grace is, verse 8 tells us, in the form of gifts, given by the ascended, ruling Lord Jesus. Verse 8 describes Him as a victorious conqueror, who has shared the spoils of His victory with His people.

• **What do verses 11-12 tell us about what these are?** They are particular abilities, which enable us to prepare each other for, or do ourselves, "works of service" (v 12). So "grace" in verse 11 is not talking about God saving us in Christ to live eternally (as it is in chapter 2), but rather, about God equipping us to be useful to Christ. His kindness is seen in Him giving us abilities in order to serve His people. We are to use our gifts for the sake of the body, the church, that it might be built up and grow.

• **How does the passage emphasise the importance of *every* Christian playing their part in their church?** The body grows as (v 16) "as each part does its work", and it is joined and held together by "every supporting ligament". Jesus has given gifts to "each" of His people (v 7), and some of those are gifts which enable and encourage others to use *their* gifts to serve (v 11-12). So Jesus has given every single Christian in every single local church a part to play in building that church. There are no spare body parts!

⊻

• **What are some examples of the different ways we can be serving in our local church?** Serving is not something reserved for full-time church workers on Sundays; or for everyone on Sundays. So it includes, for instance: hospitality; prayer; meeting up to encourage one another; speaking the truth of God's word to one another one-to-one, in small-groups, and at services; sharing the gospel with non-Christians; teaching Sunday School, running the website, administration, designing publicity, managing the church finances, playing music, cleaning…

9. The Bible calls this work of building up the church the "work of the Lord". Read 1 Corinthians 15 v 58 . What should be our attitude to this work? We should be fully devoted to it—not neglecting it or being half-hearted in it. And we should remember that it is "not in vain". The context is that because Christ rose from the dead, we will too. And so anything we do for Jesus (the "work of the Lord") is eternally significant. Though everything else will stop at death, church-building will matter for ever. Which is what motivates us to keep labouring!

⊟

• **What might stop us having this attitude, do you think?** We can be too busy with other things. Or we may simply not see this work as that important. Or we may feel we have nothing to offer. Or, of course, if we forget about the reality of death or about Christ's victory over death, then we'll either work for ourselves (forgetting death will take it all away) or not work for Jesus (forgetting that it will matter beyond death).

EXPLORE MORE
Read Matthew 9 v 38. What does Jesus say His "building project" (or harvest field) needs? More workers. The harvest is plentiful… but the workers are few. It's very easy to think it's the other way around: that the world is not a very fertile place for evangelism, and that there are plenty of

other people already doing the evangelism that is needed.
What do we need to do? Pray, asking the Lord to raise up and send out more workers.
Read 1 Corinthians 9 v 14. What is one thing we should do for people who do this work as their paid job? Support them financially through our giving. Those who do this work as their job should be freed up from having to earn their living in a regular job, so they can devote themselves to this work. Giving money to support gospel workers is a great way we can be committed to God's "building project". Like any construction project, it needs money!

10. APPLY: Why are both [edification and evangelism] important? Edification matters because God wants His people to grow to spiritual maturity and adulthood. If believers are spiritually immature, they will be vulnerable to false teaching (v 13-14). Evangelism matters because God wants all to be saved and to come to a knowledge of the truth (eg: 1 Timothy 2 v 4). If we're not committed to reaching out with the gospel, we are out of step with God.

• **What happens in a local church if we neglect one in favour of the other?** A church that neglects edification will produce spiritually immature believers who lack stability. A church that neglects evangelism will become inward-looking, will stagnate and eventually die.

• **Which do you think your church could be (or is) more in danger of not pursuing? What can you do about this?** This is not simply an opportunity to moan about your church! Remember, we've already seen that church-building is *each* Christian's job—so do focus on the second half of the question, thinking about what your group members can do.

11. APPLY: Why does the "work of the Lord" mean the Christian is never out of work? This "building project" will only be complete when Christ returns. Until that day there is always going to be work to do on it.

12. APPLY: How should this change our view of:

- **unemployment?** Although it is hard being unemployed, it is also a God-given opportunity to devote more time and energy to the "work of the Lord". As well as looking for a job, it's a chance to get more involved in serving in the local church or a mission organisation in ways we might not have been able to otherwise.

- **retirement?** Some people see retirement as a deserved chance to put their feet up and do very little; or to fritter away their final years mowing the lawn or collecting

shells on the beach; or to spend their money on long holidays. But "not having a job" is a God-given opportunity to devote more time and energy to God's "building project". The experience and maturity a retired Christian may have means they are especially well-placed to serve others.

- **weekends?** Some people see weekends as short periods of retirement! While it is right to have a time of rest each week (see next study), our weekends are times to worship God and put Him first (in works of service, and in resting). Weekends are not "our time"—if we begin to make ourselves the priority, rather than God, we will regularly skip church to go to the beach or to see friends, etc; or go straight home because the rest of the day is "ours"; and so on.

4 Hebrews 3 v 7 – 4 v 11
REST FROM WORK

THE BIG IDEA

We need to keep going in our faith so we can enjoy God's eternal rest; and we remember that rest by resting from our work now.

SUMMARY

This study has two parts. First, we look at the theme of God's rest. God's rest is revealed at three points in the Bible—at creation, at the conquest of the land, and at the coming of Christ. It is a way in which the Bible describes the kingdom of God—God's people living in His place, under His rule and blessing. This is the goal of creation. In that

sense we weren't made for work, but for rest!

Nothing is more important than that we enter God's rest. God's Old Testament people failed to enter God's rest in the land because of unbelief. The writer of Hebrews uses them as a warning to his readers, who were drifting away from the gospel. We need to keep trusting Christ, and living with Him as Lord, all the way into the eternal rest He's promised and prepared for us.

Second, we focus on rest from work. Bible-believing Christians differ over how we should rest (Every Sunday? One day a week, but not necessarily Sunday? A general pattern of getting enough rest, but not necessarily one day a week?) Whatever your views about this, the underlying principle is that we are to take time off from our work, resting properly and regularly. Scripture gives us various reasons for doing this:

- to be refreshed;
- to remember that what matters most is God's work for us;
- to listen to Jesus in His word;
- and to meet with other believers to encourage one another.

OPTIONAL EXTRA

Question One (see page 25) could easily be turned into a fun activity to start you off.

GUIDANCE FOR QUESTIONS

1. Find out what your own pace of life is by answering a few simple questions! See Study Guide, page 25. This exercise about the pace of life, developed by Professor Richard Wiseman, is meant to be a fun way of getting people to think about the theme of rest.

Score guide: how many questions did you answer "yes" to?

- None = you're so laid-back you're horizontal!
- Five = you're living in the fast lane and need to slow down before you burn out!

If you have a laptop with an internet connection, you could even do the test online with the group. Go to www.richardwiseman.com/quirkology/pace_home.htm. There are seven online questions, and you get an immediate score out of 70.

If you have the Bible passage printed out on a sheet, after the reading get the group members to circle the word "rest" every time it comes up. It will help them to see how central the theme of rest is in this passage.

• **Why are we so often so busy?** Various reasons, and all answers are "right". Some possibilities:

- There's simply a lot to do.
- Modern technology means people expect answers much more quickly and we are bombarded with lots of information.
- Busyness can be a way of proving how capable we are, to others or to ourselves. Our identity can be tied up with being busy, and being seen to be busy.
- Busyness can be a way of avoiding having time to think about deeper issues (eg: that we are sad or lonely or that a relationship is not working).

2. What was the "rest" these people failed to enter, do you think? Why didn't they get there? The "rest" was the promised land. God had promised His Old Testament people life in a land of blessing (Exodus 33 v 14). The land would be a place where they would enjoy rest from their enemies and from their journeying, and rest with God. Moses and the first generation who left Egypt failed to enter because of their unbelief and disobedience.

Note: 4 v 8 says that Joshua didn't give them rest either. This is because, although under Joshua (Moses' successor) God's people enjoyed the "rest" of living in God's place under God's rule (Joshua 21 v 44), it was not permanent rest. Because of their disobedience, God's people were thrown out of the land into exile. This rest in the promised land was only a picture of the ultimate rest.

3. What is the rest to which we are heading? Life with God in the age to come. God's "rest" is how the Bible describes the goal of everything—God's people, living in God's place under God's rule. Serving Him;

delighting in relationship with Him. This is what God's people will enjoy perfectly and for ever when Christ returns. 4 v 9 is looking forward. This is what we find in Revelation 21. (By contrast Revelation 14 v 11 says that for God's enemies "there will be no rest day or night".)

• **Why is this exciting?** What could be more thrilling than this prospect of life with God for ever in a world made new!

4. How do we enter that promised rest (3 v 19 – 4 v 3)? Through faith, believing the good news about Jesus Christ, who says: "Come to me all you who are weary and burdened, and I will give you rest" (Matthew 11 v 28).

5. What lesson should we learn from what happened to "that generation" (3 v 12-14; 4 v 1-3, 11)? Don't make the same mistake! For the believer, this passage is a warning about the need to keep going in faith. The believers to whom Hebrews was written were in danger of drifting back into unbelief, just like the Old Testament generation in the desert who failed in the end to enter God's rest. We need to keep going in gospel faith and obedience.

6. APPLY: How can we make sure that we and our fellow believers do make it to the promised rest? We each need to take care, because our hearts can become hardened by sin. To prevent this happening, we need to (literally) "exhort" one another every day. This includes encouragement and warning (in 13 v 22, the writer describes his letter as his "word of exhortation").

• **In what practical ways do you, or could you, give this and receive this?** Eg: daily Bible reading and prayer; being part of a Bible-study group; Sunday services; being in an accountability group (eg: prayer triplet); emailing and phoning and sending cards to Christian friends to encourage them. Encourage your group to be specific about themselves, with their Christian friends, in their circumstances.

7. Why did God command His Old Testament people to take a day off each week? In the Old Testament law, God commanded His people to have a day a week when they stopped working. It was important enough to make it into God's top ten at number 4!

• **Exodus 20 v 11:** To remember His work in creating them—all they had was given to them by Him. Their work was productive only because He was at work, blessing it.

• **Deuteronomy 5 v 15:** To remember that He had rescued them. They were living in the land, enjoying blessing, not because they worked hard but because they were His people. Breaking it meant effectively saying that you weren't a member of God's people, and that you weren't relying on Him.

• **Exodus 23 v 12:** Simply to have a break!

Note: In addition to the weekly Sabbath, every seventh year was to be a Sabbath year (Leviticus 25 v 3-4). And after seven Sabbath years, every 50th year was to be a special Jubilee Year in which Israel weren't to sow or reap, were to proclaim liberty for everyone, and all property was to be returned to the original owners. So the Sabbath was central to life as God's Old Testament people. Failure to observe the Sabbath could result in death for the individual (Numbers 15 v 32-35); it did result in exile for God's people (Ezekiel 20 v 12).

8. … Whatever our views on this [Sabbath] issue, what principles can we

draw from what we've learned above?
- We need rest and refreshment—it's part of being human, not machines. God has made us this way, so we need to build this rhythm of rest into our lives—each day, each week, each year. God does not recommend an annual cycle of 49 weeks of madness and 3 weeks of recovery! Without this rhythm, our lives will be imbalanced and we may burn out. We need to help each other with this. If a friend or your spouse is exhausted, we need to step in and try to help. Time off work is not something we should feel guilty about. It is part of the good life God has created for us to enjoy.
- We need time off not just to rest, but to remember that the most important thing in life is our relationship with God. We are not defined by what we do, but by this relationship with our Creator and Rescuer.

⌄

- **Read Romans 14 v 4-12. How should we treat fellow believers when we disagree about whether there is still a weekly Sabbath day?** We each need to make up our own minds from the Bible, and we mustn't judge one another when we come to different conclusions on such matters. Be aware that group members may have different and strongly-held views about whether or not Sunday is a special Sabbath day.

9. Read Luke 10 v 38-42. What did Martha need to learn about work and rest? How can we be like Martha? More important than anything we do *for* Jesus is listening *to* Jesus. We can, like Martha, be so busy doing things for Him that we don't take time to listen to Him. We need to spend time with Jesus—there is a danger

that we spend so much time working for Him that we end up very distant from Him.

- **How can we do today what Mary did then?** Jesus is now no longer with us in person, but He still speaks to us through His word, the Bible, as we read it, study it, hear it taught, and meditate on it. We're surrounded by noise—the TV and MP3. We need times when we stop emailing, surfing, texting, tweeting, and updating out status on Facebook. Times when we unplug ourselves from all our gadgets to be quiet and still, pray, and listen to Jesus in His word. It's a vital part of our daily and weekly rhythm as God's people. It's as vital to the health of our souls as sleep is for our bodies.

10. Read Hebrews 10 v 24-25. What else do we need time off work to do? To meet together regularly as God's people, to encourage one another to keep believing and keep living out our faith in a life of love and service as we look forward to meeting together. Notice that "some are in the habit of" giving up on meeting together. This is a real and live danger for us, too!

11. APPLY: In what ways will we (and those around us) suffer if we don't take seriously the need for time off work? We run the risk of burning out physically and emotionally; and of drifting away spiritually.

- **What wrong views of your life will stop you resting regularly and properly?**
- Thinking I am the centre of the universe. A refusal to rest regularly and properly may indicate I believe that the world (or my office, or church) is going to collapse if I stop. The truth is that God is in control, not me.

- Thinking I am defined by the work I do, and allowing my sense of self-worth and identity to be too closely tied to my work. My identity should be rooted in the fact that I am a child of God.
- Thinking my sense of worth is tied to my success and achievements. The truth is that God's love for me in sending his own Son to die for me shows how much I am worth.

- **What motivations to rest have the passages we've looked at given you?**
  - God made everything—He is in control, so I don't need to be.
  - God has rescued me—He has saved me and given me value and security and purpose, so I don't need to find these things elsewhere.

- God made me to rest *and* work—so it's best for me to have both in my week.
- Others need me to encourage them at church—so I need to make time to be there on Sundays, and midweek.

EXPLORE MORE
Read Heb 3 v 13. When do we need to encourage one another as believers? How could you do this? Every day. It needs to be more than just once a week at a Sunday service. Practical suggestions for more regular encouragement: sharing encouraging verses and truths by email, text, and phone; being part of a prayer triplet; meeting up one-to-one to talk and pray; being committed to a small group; setting up a Christian book-discussion group…

5 Proverbs 31
WISDOM AT WORK

THE BIG IDEA
We should live wisely at work, being godly and being wary of the pitfalls of sex, drink, and power.

SUMMARY
One of the themes of Proverbs is the practical nature of true wisdom, and this is summed up in this final chapter and the two characters we meet here. The life situations of this man and woman are very different, but there is the same emphasis on practical godliness in working life.

In verses 1-9, King Lemuel is told off by his mother for being a fool at work and misusing sex, drink, and power. But the flawed king is not the last word in Proverbs.

In verses 10-31, we are presented with perfection—a wise woman, who perfectly lives out her fear of the Lord in her working life. Verses 10-12 introduce us to her; verses 13-27 describe all her different activities; and then verses 28-31 are an invitation to join in praise of her. And so there's much to learn here in terms of "do's and don'ts" for wise living at work. But this is not just about tips for wisdom, because the "Lady Wisdom" of Proverbs (of whom the woman in chapter 31 is, it seems, an extension) points us forward to Christ, the wisest human who has ever lived, in whom is found all God's wisdom (Colossians 2 v 3). It's in knowing Christ that we find the way to live wisely in life, including at work.

OPTIONAL EXTRA

To get group members thinking about how they spend their time, and what a big part of daily life work is, you could ask them to fill in a pie-chart. They just need to draw a circle, divide it into segments and fill in how they spend their time...

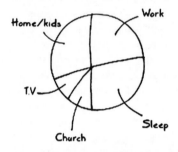

GUIDANCE FOR QUESTIONS

1. What do you make of [the "sadhu" holy men of Hinduism]? There's no questioning their commitment and dedication, but it is tragic that they are so misguided about what it means to be spiritual. The book of Proverbs teaches us that a holy life is not one in which we withdraw from the world and normal life to contemplate, but rather a life of engagement and action; a life of practical godliness in which we walk the path of wisdom in the ordinary activities of daily life, especially in our work.

2. What three things did this king seem to have a problem with? Reading between the lines, the implication is that he had a problem with sex (v 3), drink (v 4-5), and power (v 8). Note that verse 3 is not saying that women are evil and he should steer well clear of them—18 v 22 says: "He who finds a wife finds what is good and receives favour from the LORD". But on King Lemuel's radar there wasn't a wife, but

women. It seems he was a womaniser, who used his position and power to satisfy his sexual passions.

EXPLORE MORE

How is the coming King of [Isaiah 11 v 1-5] everything King Lemuel once wasn't, and everything we often fail to be too? The coming King would have "the Spirit of wisdom and understanding" and would "delight in the fear of the LORD". He would judge "with righteousness" and "with justice he will give decisions for the poor of the earth". He is the perfect Ruler, and the perfect person, who stands in marked contrast to the flawed king of Proverbs 31 and to our own sinfulness.

... How does Jesus being this kind of King encourage us: • when we see our own sinfulness? There is a perfect man who has died to save us from that sinfulness, and who has given us His Spirit to change us and enable us to live more and more wisely. What ultimately matters is not how wise or good we are, but how perfectly wise and good He is.

• **when we see our leaders' short-comings?** The newspaper all too often carries stories of the downfall of yet another leader compromised by sin. It's easy to get disillusioned with those in leadership in the workplace and the church, and with the sin in our own lives. But our leaders are not our ultimate leader now, or eternally. We can look to, live under and trust our lives to the rule of a perfect King, who never makes mistakes and who has no flaws.

3. APPLY: In what ways are the misuse of sex, drink, and power temptations for us in our working lives? The point of this question is to see how much these issues are a problem in working life today (eg: drink—the drinking culture; the work night out; drinking to deal with work stress; and so on).

In the group it may not be appropriate to share personal failings in these areas—the "Getting personal" questions provide a chance for personal reflection on sin, and for repentance. Although these are temptations with which all of us struggle (and it's good to acknowledge that), some group members may secretly be seriously compromised in one or more of these areas (eg: having an affair; addicted to pornography; alcoholic). It would be good to offer to meet one-to-one on another occasion with anyone who wants to talk further and in confidence.

4. This wise woman's working life is described in v 13-27. Make a list of her various activities. The description is of tireless activity on behalf of her household: buying (v 13, 16); making (v 15, 19, 22, 24); selling (v 24); working long hours (v 15, 18); providing for the poor (v 20); teaching her children (v 26).

- **Although her work is centred on the home, in what ways is she a bit more than what we tend to think of as a "housewife"?** This woman is an A to Z of wise living, who covers all the bases. Her making and selling give the impression she is running a small business.

5. What is driving all this activity (v 30; see also 1 v 7)? What do you think this means and doesn't mean? The fear of the LORD, which is the beginning of wisdom (1 v 7). This is an important theme in Proverbs. It means a right reverence for God, recognising that He is the all-powerful Creator and Ruler. It doesn't mean being scared stiff of Him and terrified.

6. Read Prov 6 v 6-11 and 26 v 13-16. How does this "fool" compare to the wise woman of chapter 31? She is hardworking, while one mark of the fool is laziness. The sluggard won't begin things, finish things, or face things, and comes up with ridiculous excuses for doing nothing.

7. APPLY: What does true wisdom look like in everyday life for the Christian, whether man or woman? How does true wisdom look different from the "Hindu sadhu"? This woman's life situation was very different to that of King Lemuel, but the message is the same—what God requires of His people is that we fear Him, and live that out in the ordinary business of daily working life. The ultimate is not to withdraw into a life of contemplation, but to get on with being a follower of God in your daily life and work. Wisdom wears working clothes. For the king that meant sorting out his problems with sex and drink and power, and starting to rule with integrity. For this woman it meant running her household with hard work and dedication to provide for the needs of her husband and children and the poor around her.

8. APPLY: Most of our "heroes of the faith" in church history tend to be people who have been in full-time gospel work as missionaries or church ministers or theologians. How does this passage challenge that? God's hero gallery is full of lots of ordinary Christians, like this woman, living out their faith and fear of the Lord in the nitty-gritty of everyday life and work.

Note: The word "noble" in verse 10 is used elsewhere in the Bible to describe male warriors in phrases such as "mighty men of war". The idea that this woman is a heroic warrior is seen also in references to her strength (v 17, 25). This hard-working woman running her household is the female equivalent of the male warrior going into battle and returning a conquering hero!

9. APPLY: … How could you encourage [Sarah] from this passage? And if you were her husband, how would v 28-31 challenge you? In God's sight the godly, hardworking mother at home is a heroine. You could encourage her to see herself as God sees her rather than how her friends see her.

Her husband should praise her and make clear to her how much he values what she is doing. Sometimes husbands are guilty of just taking for granted what their wives do; or they even actively discourage them from such a role, letting their values be shaped more by the world than by the word.

⯆

• **Is it wrong for a Christian woman to "go out to work".** Some women will need to "go out to work", because they don't have a family to raise or household to run, or because it is a financial necessity. However, while acknowledging this, we also mustn't ignore the important place running a household has in the Bible (1 Timothy 5 v 14; Titus 2 v 4). It is very striking that to end this book about wise living, the model God leaves us with to sum everything up is not a warrior, not a ruler, but a hard-working woman whose work is centred on the home. Bear in mind this issue about gender roles may be a very sensitive one in the group. And bear in mind, too, that it is possible to become legalistic about this area. Christians are at liberty to work out what is wise for them, with their particular character and circumstances. Other Christians are *not* at liberty to make rules and impose them.

10. [Read Colossians 2 v 3.] What will this wise choice look like for us, living in the twenty-first century rather than in Old Testament Israel? The wisdom of God finds its fullest expression and embodiment in Jesus. So wisdom will mean that we choose to trust and follow Him, the wisdom of God; and that as those who know Him we walk the path of wisdom, fearing the Lord, serving Him in the day-to-day of working life as we were created to do.

11. APPLY: "In God's sight, wisdom is more important than intelligence." What do you make of this statement? What are its implications? Someone who is not a Christian may be highly intelligent, but in God's sight they are a fool because they have not accepted Jesus, in whom God's wisdom is revealed. Equally, intelligent Christians are not always wise Christians. And someone who is a Christian may not be at all academically able, but in God's sight they are wise because they trust Christ, listen to Christ, and seek intentionally in every situation to live for and like Christ.

So in our churches, small groups, etc, we also need to make sure we value wisdom more than intelligence. We mustn't look down on those who are less intelligent or put on a pedestal those who are more intelligent. Instead, we should praise and hold up as role-models those who are wise—people who fear the Lord and are living that out in everyday life. God's hero gallery contains lots of simple, ordinary, godly folk.

6 Colossians 3 v 22 – 4 v 6
WITNESS AT WORK

THE BIG IDEA
Whatever we're doing, we can and should do it for God; and we can and should be telling those around us about His Son.

SUMMARY
These instructions to first-century Christian slaves and masters (3 v 22 – 4 v 1) are the closest thing we have in the Bible to instructions about working life. They come in a section about submitting to authority in various relationships (wives-husbands, children-fathers, slaves-masters). The distinctive motivation for the Christian at work is that we are serving the Lord and working for Him. We are to be obedient to the boss, conscientious, wholehearted, and patient, looking to our heavenly reward.

The second half of the passage (4 v 2-6) contains general instructions, but these too can be applied to the workplace. We are to be devoted to prayer, praying for God to open doors for us to share the gospel and for us to be clear as we do so. Even though there may be a cost involved, we are graciously to make the most of every opportunity, and to be ready to respond to questions people may ask.

OPTIONAL EXTRA
Game: *Spot the Difference*. There are lots of these games online, where you have to spot the differences between two pictures. Playing this game sets up the issue of in what way the Christian is to be different in the workplace. It's actually quite challenging to ask ourselves: Is there any real, noticeable difference between me and my non-Christian co-workers?

GUIDANCE FOR QUESTIONS
1. "Preach the gospel. Use words if necessary." What do you agree and/or disagree with in this statement?
Agree: We are to share the gospel with others. And how we live as Christians is important to our witness.
Disagree: Words are not an optional extra in sharing the gospel. They are necessary. The gospel is a message of good news which people need to hear, understand, and believe to be saved. Others cannot figure out the gospel message by just looking at how a Christian lives.
If there is some disagreement within the group (or the whole group disagrees with the answer here!), you could move on to Q2 and then return to this question after Q12.

2. How should the Christian behave at work? How do you think this behaviour might contrast with how others behave at work? Be obedient to the boss, not disrespectful; be conscientious, not only working hard when the boss is around; be wholehearted, doing your best, not being half-hearted and just doing your duty; be patient, not just working for a salary but for heavenly reward, and keep going in the face of injustice in the workplace, knowing the wrongdoer will be repaid one day. And if you are the boss, then treat others as you want your heavenly Master to treat you.

3. Which phrases refer to the motivation for behaving this way at work? We do it for the Lord, to serve Him, not just because we want promotion—with "reverence for the Lord" (v 22), "as working for the Lord" (v 23); "it is the Lord Christ you are serving" (v 25). Masters remember about God, too; they also "have a Master in heaven" (4 v 1). This is the engine of Christian behaviour. We're not doing it to earn salvation, but for the Lord who has rescued us. The Christian won't be the only person who submits to the boss and works hard, but the Christian motivation is unique.

4. If someone is in a job where they have people working for them, how should they behave? 4 v 1: they should provide them "with what is right and fair" ie: treat them well; reward them fairly.

5. APPLY: It's easy to forget about the Lord in the busyness of work. What can we do to help us keep Him at the centre of all we do during a working day? Ideas could include:

- Set aside some time for reading the Bible and praying before work each day, so that you go into the working day having heard from the Lord and having spoken to Him.
- Write out a verse from that day's reading on a piece of paper to have in your pocket as a reminder.
- Take five minutes during the working day to go somewhere quiet and pray.
- Arrange to meet regularly for a few minutes with another Christian who works nearby, to encourage one another spiritually and pray together.
- Whenever you're faced with a dull to-do list, write "FTL" ("For the Lord") next to the worst item and do it for Him.
- Work at getting into the habit of saying short prayers to the Lord during the working day as you face particular challenges and pressures.

6. APPLY: We are not being told to be workaholics or perfectionists! What difference is there between godliness and workaholism? How do you tell which you are, do you think? The perfectionist believes that any work they do must be perfect, or they can't accept themselves and they think others won't accept them either, and they're overcome by guilt and anxiety. But as Christians, we work for a heavenly Boss, who fully accepts us in Christ, even before our working day begins. And as Christians, our starting-point is that we're sinners, and so we're not trying to keep up an illusion of being perfect.
The workaholic has work out of perspective. They look to work for their sense of self-worth and identity, and everything else comes second to work. The godly person works hard but gets their self-worth from being loved by God. They recognise that work is just one of many responsibilities God has given them.

7. APPLY: Share any encouraging stories of people noticing that Christians are different at work, either from your own experience or that of others you know. Two true stories just in case you're stuck!

- The council road-sweeper where we live was a Christian man called Julius. One day I was outside the house and I was struck by how friendly he was and that he offered to clean part of our driveway, although it's not in his brief. A while later, some locals got together and gave him a surprise award. This is what one of them said in the newspaper article about him: "During the snow we had last winter, he cleared the pavements even though he didn't have to. He always says good morning and has time for a chat with any resident. We think he's great." If the way someone does his street-sweeping is noticed, how much more so if you spend 40 hours a week with the same people!

• In the book *Thank God It's Monday*, Mark Greene tells the story of Emily, a small Chinese Christian lady working at the United Nations. One day one of her co-workers, a fairly large lady, wasn't feeling well. "Can I get you a cup of tea?" Emily enquired. "No" the other replied rather abruptly. "I don't like the tea here. I only drink camomile." Emily left her, quietly slipped on her coat, took the lift down several floors and went down the street to a nearby shop. She returned with a box of camomile tea and gave it in her small hand to this large lady, who immediately enveloped her in a huge hug, exclaiming: "Emily, I love you"!

It is worth saying that these two (and many others) are positive stories about being distinctive at work as Christians. Of course, there will also be times when we live differently at work and are criticised or disliked for it—eg: not joining in with gossip or coarse joking; refusing to abuse our timesheet or expenses account; not making our job the centre of our lives; etc.

EXPLORE MORE

Read Titus 2 v 9-10. What motivation is given here for godly behaviour at work? What does that mean?

Read Matthew 5 v 16. How is Titus 2 confirming what Jesus teaches here?

Godly behaviour makes the gospel message attractive to non-Christians. It shows them that it works and makes a difference and isn't just words. Jesus says that the way Christians behave should be like a light in a dark place, pointing people to the Father and leading them to praise Him too.

Why do people need to know we are Christian, as well as seeing us behave as Christians? When we don't live distinctively, it reflects badly on the gospel, whereas when we are living distinctively, it commends the gospel to others and makes it attractive. So our behaviour at work really matters. The credibility of the gospel is at stake. Would you buy a work-out DVD if the instructor on the front looked like a sack of potatoes?! If the gospel hasn't changed us, why would others be interested?

But people will only make this link between our lives and the gospel if they know we're Christian. If they don't know, it's like watching a great TV advertisement which never mentions the name of the product. You wouldn't know what to buy! People will just think what a nice person you are.

8. What two things did Paul ask for prayer about?

• v 3: For God to open a door for the gospel message (a door of opportunity for the gospel to be explained, and the door of hearts to be open to receive that word).
• v 4: To be clear in explaining the message.

• **Why do you think we too need to pray this?** Only if God is at work will anything we say have any lasting effect. We need Him to open the doors of opportunities and to give us the right words to say, and so we need to pray for that. If Paul needed help with this, how much more do we! And by praying such prayers we will actually be more alert to opportunities when they come.

9. What does verse 5 say about people, and about time? How does this help us?

Most of those we work with are "outsiders" (v 4)—outside the kingdom, without eternal life. They need to hear the gospel. Who is going to tell them if we don't? So we need to make the most of every opportunity. Literally, v 5 reads: "buying up the time". Time is short. Christ is coming soon. There is an urgency in passing on the gospel.

10. The phrase "know how to answer" (v 6) implies that people will ask questions. What do you think might prompt people to do that? Distinctive gospel behaviour does get noticed and may lead to questions (see also 1 Peter 3 v 15). They may ask why you don't fiddle your expenses like everyone else, why you aren't you living with your boyfriend, why you don't get drunk. Or they may ask why you do go to church, why you helped someone out, why you didn't try to get your own back when someone wronged you.

11. APPLY: The phrase "for which I am in chains" reminds us that sharing the gospel is a costly business. What do you think that cost might look like for you, in your workplace? Speaking the gospel landed Paul in prison. For us, sharing the gospel at work may ruffle some feathers, get you labelled, leave you outside the "in" crowd, or lose you a promotion. You may even lose your job.

☷

- **Why not just keep quiet, then?!** The need for non-Christians to hear the gospel is too great for us to keep quiet. And an attitude of "not mentioning the gospel

because it might get me in trouble" is alien to New Testament Christianity. Jesus said: "Whoever wants to be my disciple must deny themselves and take up their cross…" (Mark 8 v 34). In the Bible we find believers, when told to be quiet, saying they need to obey God rather than man (Acts 4 v 18-20), risking everything for the gospel—their freedom, families, even life itself. Our allegiance to Christ will make us stand out in the workplace, but ultimately we are working for the Lord and need to obey Him, trusting that He'll provide for all our needs as we do that.

12. APPLY: This passage has taught us both to live out the gospel life and pass on the gospel message. What would happen if we did the first, but not the second? People would like you and think you are a very nice person, but they wouldn't be prompted to take Jesus seriously, because they wouldn't know *why* you live as you do.

- **What would happen if you did the second, but not the first?** People would be put off the gospel and dismiss Christians as hypocrites who don't practise what they preach.

7 1 Timothy 6 v 6-10, 17-19
MONEY AND WORK

THE BIG IDEA
Our contentment should come from knowing God, not having money—and so we can be generous with all that we have.

SUMMARY
These two passages on money come after a section dealing with false teachers. 1 Timothy 6 v 5 ends by describing the false teachers as those "who think that godliness

is a means to financial gain". Paul then picks up this idea of "gain" in v 6, in speaking of the value of contentment.

The first section (v 6-10) could be summed up as "work to live". We are to be content with life's essentials (which we usually provide for ourselves, through the money we earn at work), instead of being covetous. Paul warns about the spiritual dangers of loving money.

The second section (v 17-19) could be summed up as "work to give". Paul commands those who are rich to be thankful and generous, these being some of the fruits of true faith.

This is a study in which the passages are not particularly hard to understand; what is far harder is applying them to our lives in a humble, honest, trusting way.

GUIDANCE FOR QUESTIONS

1. What is the connection between work and money? This question is to help people to see why a study on money is part of a series on work. One reason we work is to earn money. It's not the only reason but an important one. It's part of how God intends society to function. Not all work gets paid—the work of the housewife, voluntary work, the gospel work we all do as believers—but for most jobs the deal is that you work and you get pay in return.

2. What attitude do verses 6-8 urge us to have? Why? To be godly and content with what we have. When it comes to money and possessions, we should be content to have life's essentials—food to eat, clothes to wear, and a roof over our heads. There is great gain in such contentment. We brought nothing into the world with us when we were born, and won't take anything with us when we die. There's more

to life than money and things. As people, we are not defined by our income, car, or house. You were you before you had any of it, and will still be you when you leave it all behind. Problems start when we lose this perspective, our identity becomes tied to our income and possessions, and we look to these things for our sense of worth, thinking: "I am what I earn or drive".

⌄

- **What if we have more or less than these essentials?** Having less than these essentials, living in poverty, is not a good thing, and we should be helping those who don't have these essentials to get them. Having more than these essentials isn't wrong, but shouldn't be necessary to be content. There are great spiritual challenges both in experiencing poverty and wealth (see Proverbs 30 v 8).

3. How is the desire to get rich harmful (v 9-10)? Those who desire to be rich fall into temptation, a trap laid by the devil, and many foolish and harmful desires: envy, as you try to keep up with the neighbours; selfish ambition; worry, as you fret about your savings and possessions; dissatisfaction, because the love of money is addictive. The more you have, the more you want (Ecclesiastes 5 v 10). The love of money never satisfies. It corrodes character; messes us up as people; and causes spiritual ruin, both now and in eternity. Those who set their hearts on gain end in total loss—loss of integrity now and of themselves in eternity. God sticks a big spiritual health warning on the love of money. **What might this look like in 21st-century life?** Some pursue the dream of greater riches through crime, some through gambling (eg: the Lottery), and some through work. They dream of getting a better car or bigger house, being able to go on better holidays, or retiring early and having no financial worries for the future.

4. "The love of money is a root of all kinds of evil" (v 10) is sometimes misquoted as "money is the root of all evil". There are three differences. What are they? Why are they important?
- It's the *love of* money, not money (money in itself is a good gift to be used for good).
- It's *a* root, not *the* root (love of money is not the only sin we need to beware).
- It's a root of *all kinds* of evils, not *all* evil (not all evil can be traced back to the love of money. There are many other roots of evil, eg: pride, selfishness, lust).

5. Read Matthew 6 v 24. How do Paul's words to Timothy echo Jesus' warning here? You cannot serve both God and Money. Either we love money and make it the god we serve, or we love the Lord and serve Him—but we can't do both. So Jesus' words in Matthew 6 would make a good summary statement of Paul's teaching in 1 Timothy 6.

6. APPLY: How does advertising fuel the love of money, and rob us of contentment? Advertising is not in itself wrong, but it can fan the flame of these wrong desires. Advertisers have been called "merchants of discontent". They tempt us to imagine what life would be like "if only you had this product". And glossy magazines invite us into the homes and lives of celebrities and sow seeds of discontent, so that we think: "I need what I don't have—I must go and buy it!" or: "If only my standard of living were higher!"

7. APPLY: Why do we try to serve God and money? Some of us may know it's

wrong, but think we can get away with it; that we can have our cake and eat it. But many Christians simply do not see it as being an issue. Some churches teach that God wants us to be wealthy. Even in churches where that isn't the case, the love of money is so accepted and encouraged in the world around us, we may not even be aware of how wrong some of our desires and expectations are. And the materialism of fellow Christians can make us think it is acceptable.

In some churches, there is an embarrassment in talking about money, which means the subject gets avoided and wrong attitudes are never challenged. Church pastors may avoid the issue because they don't want to upset people who are giving to support the church. And sometimes we are so focused on other sins (such as sexual immorality) that we ignore this one.

- **Is your church a place in which the love of money is being challenged? Are your Christian friendships places where the love of money, in yourself and others, is challenged?**

8. APPLY: What might be some signs that we do love money? What action should we take if we do? One test is how generous you are (more of this in v 17-19). That you are generous in giving money away is a sign that it does not have a hold on you. The "Getting Personal" questions are designed to help explore this more. Ultimately it is a heart problem, which needs a heart solution—a greater love for God in place of the love of money. But there are practical steps we can take—making a budget; sorting out our giving; being accountable to others.

- **How would you want others to react if they noticed it in you?** Of course, the "right answer" is: to speak to me about it. But it's worth gently challenging the group as to whether that's the *real* answer. Often, we'd rather people didn't mention our sin to us; we show that to be the case whenever we react to someone gently rebuking us defensively or angrily, or by attacking them.

EXPLORE MORE
Read Luke 16 v 14-15. What is surprising here? Jesus condemns the Pharisees as lovers of money. The love of money can be found in the most unexpected places, including in people who outwardly appear righteous and godly, like the Pharisees. **Read 2 Thessalonians 3 v 7-12. How should we treat someone who refuses to work to provide for themselves? What if someone is unable to work or to find work?** If a person refuses to work, we shouldn't support them. The scrounger who refuses to work needs to stop sponging off others or the state and look for a job. If they are unable to work or unable to find work, that's a different matter, but if they are just idle and refuse to work, that is wrong. One way we serve God in His world, loving Him and others, is that we work to provide for life's essentials and pay our way, supporting ourselves rather than depending on others.

9. For those who are rich, what are:
- **the dangers?** v 17: Riches can make us proud, self-important, and we look down on others who have less. With money comes influence and respect. And wealth can bring a false sense of security. We can end up trusting in money instead of in God. But it is so uncertain, and at best lasts only for this life.

- **the duties?** v 18: With wealth comes the responsibility to be generous—in hospitality, sharing our homes and possessions, and in giving money to those in need and to gospel work.

- **incentives for performing those duties?** v 19: If we are content and generous as God's people, we are storing up treasure in heaven, showing evidence of true faith in the God who has been so generous to us as our Creator and Redeemer. But if, instead, we are covetous, self-indulgent and stingy, we should be concerned and we need to repent. These are not the fruits of true faith.

⌄

- **Is it wrong to be rich?** See 4 v 1-5. Good things are gifts from God, to be received and enjoyed humbly and thankfully. The Bible never criticises a wealthy person for being wealthy; it criticises some wealthy people for how they use that wealth. So rich people are not wrong to be rich, but they are wrong if they don't thank God for His good gifts, don't beware the dangers of pride and trusting in wealth, or fail to give generously. The problem is not money, but the love of money.

10. APPLY: Imagine that someone at church says to you: "I don't have a problem with money. I give 10% of my income to the church." How would you respond? Giving away 10% of your income is no guarantee that you don't have a problem with money. Many Christians are wealthy enough that giving away 10% still leaves them with plenty to live a life of luxury. Even when that's not the case, you could still love money—spending the other 90% selfishly and dreaming of greater riches. And anyway, 10% was just the Old Testament command. Now that Christ has come and we are no longer under that law, should we not be even more generous?

OPTIONAL EXTRA

After the study, play a few rounds of *Monopoly* (a full game takes too long!), and ask how the game teaches the same point as these passages. In Monopoly, you can be doing very well, with lots of money and property, but things can suddenly change and you lose it all. And in the end, when the game's over, it all goes back in the box. It doesn't really matter who wins. It's the same in life. Life is so uncertain (v 17)—you can go from having everything to losing it all very quickly. And when you die, it all goes back in the box—game over (v 7). Unlike *Monopoly,* though, what we do with these things during our lives matters, and is of eternal significance. It's not just a game (v 19).

8 Matthew 6 v 25-34
WORRY AT WORK

THE BIG IDEA

Stop worrying about work, because fretting is needless, pointless, and godless. God is good, and has it all under control!

SUMMARY

This is part of the Sermon on the Mount, in which Jesus teaches His disciples about how to live as members of His kingdom. These verses are about worry, and how to deal with it. Though not specifically about work-related worry, the principles can be applied to the office, home, and everywhere else!

The command "do not worry" comes up three times (v 25, 31, 34). Jesus knows our tendency to be anxious about life, and here provides us with the tools for dealing with it. His three lessons could be summed up as:

- Worry is needless: trust God's fatherly care (v 26, 28-30).
- Worry is pointless: remember God's sovereign control (v 27,34).
- Worry is godless: seek God's eternal kingdom (v 31-33).

GUIDANCE FOR QUESTIONS

1. What kind of work things do people worry about? This could be done in pairs—see who can come up with the longest list in three minutes, and then feed back to the group. Some answers: long working hours; a particular task or meeting; deadlines; too much to do; feeling that you're not making the grade, either set by others or that you set yourself; lack of support and feeling isolated; fear of losing your job; being badly treated by others at work; not getting on with someone. **In what different ways does work-related worry affect people?** If you've had a stressful day at work you may just feel exhausted, a bit low, preoccupied. But as you move along the scale the symptoms get more severe. All-consuming anxiety; the feeling that things are hanging over you; poor concentration and difficulty in making decisions; sleep problems; excessive caffeine intake; headaches. And then you get to the stage of pounding heart and palpitations; loss of appetite for food and sex; depression. And finally the stage when you feel you just can't cope and lose all sense of perspective, and have a breakdown.

2. What reason does Jesus give for not worrying in verse 25? What does He mean? There's more to life than material things such as food and the body and clothing and other things that we worry about. Jesus doesn't just mean that we have family and friends as well, but rather, that life is ultimately about our relationship with God the Father and His eternal kingdom (v 33), not just the things we see around us.

3. What do the birds and flowers teach us (v 26, 28-30)? How does Jesus' description of His disciples in verse 30 show they needed this lesson? Birds teach us about God's loving care. God looks after them, feeds them, provides for them. We are infinitely more precious to God than a sparrow. And so if God looks after the birds, how much more will He look after us. That's not to say we don't need to work. We do—God uses our efforts to provide for us (as we saw in Study One). But rather than fretting, we can trust our heavenly Father. Flowers are here today, gone tomorrow, whereas we are eternal. If God clothes the grass so beautifully, how much more will He clothe us and provide for our needs! Fretting about life betrays a lack of trust in our heavenly Father. Jesus rebukes His disciples for this: "You of little faith" (v 30).

4. APPLY: … How could you use this truth of our heavenly Father's care to comfort [Mike]? You could ask her if she thinks God cares more about birds and flowers than about her! You could assure her that she has a loving heavenly Father who cares for her. You could encourage her

to trust Him and to entrust to Him all her worries and cares, knowing that He watches over her, cares for her, and will provide for her. You could offer to pray with her about these things.

Remedy One = Trust God's fatherly care.

EXPLORE MORE
Read Philippians 4 v 6-7. What are we to do with our worries? Pray about them, bringing our requests to God.
What assurance is given to encourage us to do this? He promises to give us peace in our hearts as we do this.
What things keep us from doing this more? Sometimes we don't pray because we think our worries are too small to bother God with. But if they're big enough to worry about, they're big enough to pray about!

5. In verses 27 and 34, Jesus gives two reasons why there is no point in worrying. What are they?
• Worrying doesn't achieve anything. It can't make us live longer.
• There's enough on our plates to worry about today, without bringing in the concerns of tomorrow as well. Worrying about tomorrow is a pointless waste of time and energy. Who knows what tomorrow may bring? And so often the things we worry about turn out differently when the day comes.

6. APPLY: The future is *not* in our hands; it *is* in God's. How does knowing these are both true help us? It means we can relax, knowing He is in control. We may be worried about our work future and fear losing our jobs, and feel that it's out of our hands. It is! But it's never out of God's hands! Sometimes when we're worrying, we can feel that we're carrying the world on our shoulders. But that's God's job. We need to let Him do His job, and not try to do it for Him! Nothing can happen to us apart from His will.

7. APPLY: In what sense are we to live "one day at a time"? Where does that leave planning for the future, do you think? Many of the things we worry about are in the future. We don't know the future and can't control it, but we know the One who holds the future in His hands! We are to get on with living for God today. Jesus is not saying we shouldn't make plans for tomorrow or provide for tomorrow—the ant in Proverbs 6 v 6-8 is considered wise for storing up provisions in the summer for the winter time—but we're not to worry about tomorrow. We are free to focus on enjoying today, and on serving God today, knowing He already has tomorrow under control.

Remedy Two = Remember God's sovereign control.

EXPLORE MORE
Read Matthew 10 v 29-30. What does Jesus teach about God's control over our lives? The circumstances and details of our lives are in God's hands. He has it all planned out, even down to the date you will die. If even the fate of a sparrow is in God's hands, how much more so the details of our lives. Worry can be a control issue—we want to control everything. But actually we deal with worry by recognising that we're not in control, but God is.
Read Philippians 2 v 20; 4 v 6. In the original Greek, "genuine concern" and "anxious" are the same word. So what would you say is the difference between a right concern and a wrong worry? Timothy is praised as someone who is concerned for others. That is a good and

godly concern. We're not to be people who have a "what do I care?" attitude. But we are not to worry and fret. The same word is used negatively and positively.

8. What does Jesus say non-Christians run after (v 31-33)? Food, drink and clothing. **Why does He choose the phrase "run after", do you think?** You only "run after" what you really want, what you think you must have. So the pagan (ie: non-Christian world) lives as if these material things are the most important things in life. Such good gifts from God become idols when we live for them and make them ultimate things.

9. In what way should the priorities of Jesus' followers be different? The contrast here is very deliberate. Literally, we're not to seek after these things, but rather, seek first the kingdom of God and His righteousness. While the world around is absorbed in its trivial pursuits, we are to seek first the kingdom. We're not to detach ourselves from material things and reject them as if they were evil, but we recognise that there is more to life—there is God and His kingdom, and living to please Him. **What does that mean?** That we are concerned that more and more people enter that kingdom, through hearing and believing the gospel; and are committed to serving those in the kingdom in a local church; and living not just for now but for the eternal future. Seeking His righteousness will mean being committed to growing in godliness, in Christ-like character. It's not about turning our backs on material things but about our priority. The kingdom is what we are to seek first, above all else.

10. APPLY: How do advertisements and the titles of glossy magazines show that

the things people chase after has not changed much since the 1st century? The titles of popular magazines hold up a mirror to what people think most important—*Food & Fashion, Health & Fitness; Homes & Gardens; Cars & Bikes; Ideal Home; Interiors.* Non-Christians pursue these things, and worry about having or keeping them as if this was what life was all about.

11. APPLY: What might it look like to "seek first his kingdom" in your workplaces? To do your work as for the Lord, serving Him. To live out your faith in a godly life. To pray for and seek opportunities to share the gospel. To encourage other Christians at work in their faith. To deal with worry in a godly way, putting this study into practice! You could encourage your group to discuss what these things would look like in the specific realities of their workplaces.

☒

• **Can you seek first the kingdom *and* be ambitious at work?** We need to ask: *Is it my ambition to get promotion because I want to be the best I can be in serving God in His world, making the most of the gifts He has given me to serve Him, and be a godly influence over more people?* If so, then it could be part of seeking God's kingdom. But if it is just because I want to prove myself and show I'm the best, or to get more money and power and status, then it is selfish ambition. Ambition is not wrong in itself; the question is whether we're ambitious for God to be glorified, or for ourselves to be respected/richer/etc.

Remedy Three = Seek God's eternal kingdom.

12. APPLY: Think over what we've seen the Bible says about work. What changes to your attitude or actions are you prompted to make? Encourage people to think and write down their answers, and then to share them with the group. You might like to open your time of prayer by lifting up these changes to God, asking for His help.

OPTIONAL EXTRA

There are a number of hymns and songs which relate to the theme of this session. At the end you could listen to one or more of them, or sing them, or just print off the words and read them:

• *What a friend we have in Jesus* (about the peace that comes from carrying everything to God in prayer)

• *I do not know what lies ahead* (about God holding the future)

• *One day at a time, sweet Jesus* (about living a day at a time).

A selection from the Good Book Guide series...

OLD TESTAMENT

Ruth: Poverty and plenty
4 studies. ISBN: 9781905564910

1 Kings: The rise and fall of King Solomon 8 studies.
ISBN: 9781907377976

NEW! Esther: Royal rescue
7 studies. ISBN: 9781908317926

Ezekiel: The God of glory
6 studies. ISBN: 9781904889274

NEW! Hosea: God's love song
8 studies. ISBN: 9781905564255

Jonah: The depths of grace
6 studies. ISBN: 9781907377433

NEW TESTAMENT

Mark 1 – 8: The coming King
10 studies. ISBN: 9781904889281

1 Corinthians 10 – 16: Loving church
8 studies. ISBN: 9781908317964

Galatians: Gospel matters
7 studies. ISBN: 9781908762559

Ephesians: God's big plan
10 studies. ISBN: 9781907377099

1 Peter: Living in the real world
5 studies. ISBN: 9781904889496

1 John: How to be sure
7 studies. ISBN: 9781904889953

Revelation 2 – 3: A message from Jesus to the church today
7 studies. ISBN: 9781905564682

TOPICAL

Biblical womanhood 10 studies.
ISBN: 9781904889076

Man of God 10 studies.
ISBN: 9781904889977

Promises kept: Bible overview
9 studies. ISBN: 9781908317933

Experiencing God 6 studies.
ISBN: 9781906334437

Contentment 6 studies.
ISBN: 9781905564668

I Believe: The Apostles' Creed
10 studies. ISBN: 9781905564415

Visit your friendly neighbourhood website to see the full range, and to download samples
• **UK & Europe:** www.thegoodbook.co.uk • **USA & Canada:** www.thegoodbook.com •
• **Australia:** www.thegoodbook.com.au • **New Zealand:** www.thegoodbook.co.nz •

For more on how to let the gospel shape the way you think and feel about work…

GOSPEL CENTRED
WORK
Becoming the worker God wants you to be

Tim Chester

Tim Chester is a pastor in the Crowded House church-planting network in Sheffield, UK. He is a popular speaker and author.

Chapters on pressure and stress, worry, fear, failure, workaholism and how to get on with difficult colleagues

• • •

Lots of practical application

• • •

Ideal for self study or with a small group

thegoodbook
COMPANY

At The Good Book Company, we are dedicated to helping Christians and local churches grow. We believe that God's growth process always starts with hearing clearly what He has said to us through His timeless word—the Bible.

Ever since we opened our doors in 1991, we have been striving to produce resources that honour God in the way the Bible is used. We have grown to become an international provider of user-friendly resources to the Christian community, with believers of all backgrounds and denominations using our Bible studies, books, evangelistic resources, DVD-based courses and training events.

We want to equip ordinary Christians to live for Christ day by day, and churches to grow in their knowledge of God, their love for one another, and the effectiveness of their outreach.

Call us for a discussion of your needs or visit one of our local websites for more information on the resources and services we provide.

UK & Europe: www.thegoodbook.co.uk
North America: www.thegoodbook.com
Australia: www.thegoodbook.com.au
New Zealand: www.thegoodbook.co.nz

UK & Europe: 0333 123 0880
North America: 866 244 2165
Australia: (02) 6100 4211
New Zealand (+64) 3 343 1990

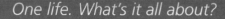